W9-BFR-245

For Christian Schools

SPELLING

By Sound and Structure

Grade 4

Rod and Staff Publishers, Inc.
P.O. Box 3, Hwy. 172
Crockett, Kentucky 41413
Telephone: (606) 522-4348

Acknowledgements

We acknowledge the everlasting God, the Lord, beside whom there is none else. His blessing made the writing and publishing of this book possible.

We express gratitude to Brother John David Martin for writing this revision, Brothers Bennie Hostetler and Marvin Eicher for editing, Brothers Marvin Good and John Dale Yoder for reviewing, and Sisters Amy Herr and Christine Collins for artwork.

We are grateful for the teachers and students who tested this revision in their classrooms and for all those who helped to make this book possible.

ISBN 978-07399-0701-6

Catalog no. 164912

Outline of Concepts

A Sounds and Letters
B Using Your Words
C Building Words

Teacher Introduction

THE IMPORTANCE OF SPELLING IN A LANGUAGE

God has given man the ability to send messages by writing. The written word can be sent to people far away from the author. A written message can also be preserved over long periods of time. The written word can help to preserve a language as writers adhere to the prescribed rules governing the system that characterizes a given language.

Spelling is a vital part of the system of a language. For a message to be conveyed accurately, the writer and the reader must both be familiar with the same set of rules that dictate the forming of discernible words or word parts. Should someone write *oshin*, the reader may have difficulty understanding that he is referring to one of the large bodies of water on the earth. Spelling rules will help students to represent the various sounds in a word with the correct letters.

While the phonetic approach to reading is good, students sometimes have difficulty translating phonetic sounds into standard spellings. For that reason, the revised *Spelling by Sound and Structure* emphasizes the interpretation of phonetic spellings. The student is also required to write the words from the spelling lists a number of times throughout his work. The exposure that a student receives simply by writing a word repeatedly will help to rivet the proper spelling in his mind. The primary goal is finally to teach the student the standard spellings of the words in the word lists, both by the use of spelling rules and by rote, as well as to give him practice with using those words intelligently.

Proper pronunciation is vital to good spelling skills. If a person has a habit of mispronouncing certain words, he may spell those words the way he says them. For example, if one says *travlin* for *traveling*, he may fail to insert an *e* between the *v* and *l*. Saying *excape* for *escape* is another example of careless speech that may hinder proper spelling.

ORGANIZATION OF *SPELLING BY SOUND AND STRUCTURE*

This book has thirty-four lessons divided into units of six lessons each except for the last unit, which has only four lessons. Each unit (except the last) has five regular lessons followed by a review lesson for that unit. The units are generally self-contained, so that a student can find the spelling rules and helps for each review lesson within the same unit.

Each regular lesson has sixteen NEW WORDS and four REVIEW WORDS. Each lesson is divided into three main parts.

Part A, Sounds and Letters, drills the phonetic composition of the words in the spelling list. Spelling rules for the speech sounds taught in the lesson are given just before the work relating to them. In many of the lessons, students will need to interpret a number of phonetic spellings.

Part B, Using Your Words, emphasizes the vocabulary aspect of the spelling words. In most lessons, students must use spelling words to fill in the blanks in a paragraph and to write two original sentences. These original sentences should have substance and show that the student is able to use the words intelligently. Part B also teaches skills such as alphabetical order and word meanings. As with the other lesson parts, the student is expected to use the *Speller Dictionary* as needed.

Part C, Building Words, emphasizes the use of words or word parts in forming other words. Syllable divisions, plural and compound nouns, verb forms, abbreviations, prefixes and suffixes, and contractions are some of the concepts taught. Some lessons also contain a section entitled *Dictionary Practice*, which teaches basic dictionary skills.

An additional part at the end of each lesson is entitled *Bible Thoughts*. This part is designed to link the spelling words to Bible concepts. The student is to use his Bible as needed in completing this part.

LESSON PLANS FOR *SPELLING BY SOUND AND STRUCTURE*

If spelling class is scheduled only once in a week, the test for the prior week's words should be given first. The new lesson should then be assigned. The teacher should read the spelling words to the students or have the students read the words with him. This is essential so that the students learn the correct pronunciation of the words.

The written work should be assigned as homework. The teacher could discuss with the students any concepts that he thinks may be difficult for them. However, the students should be able to do most of the work by themselves. A second spelling test may be given at the discretion of the teacher.

If spelling class is scheduled two times per week, one class period could be used to correct the regular work and give the first spelling test. The second class could be used to discuss the work more thoroughly, give the second spelling test, and assign the new lesson.

SPELLING TESTS

After pupils have completed the work in the spelling lesson and have studied the words in the word lists sufficiently, the spelling test should be administered. If pupils are having problems with mastering the words, a trial test given a day or two before the final test may be desirable.

Testing procedures other than the ones suggested below may be acceptable if the results accurately portray the degree of word mastery.

Administering the Spelling Test

Use the test sentences provided with each lesson. Pronounce the word once, say the sentence, and pronounce the word again. The pupils will write only the words for numbers 1–16.

To test the REVIEW WORDS, you may elect to have the pupils write the entire sentence that contains two of the REVIEW WORDS. If using this method, say the sentence carefully twice before the pupils begin to write them.

Every sixth lesson reviews the words from the preceding five lessons. To test these lessons, use the test sentences provided if time permits. Be sure that pupils understand that they are to write only abbreviations for the specified words.

Scoring the Test

For tests from the regular lessons, you could apply 100 points and deduct 5 points for each misspelled word to get a percent grade. If you have pupils write the entire sentences for the REVIEW WORDS, deduct 5 points for any misspelled REVIEW WORDS in those sentences and 1 point for any other misspelled words in the sentence. Never deduct more than 10 points per sentence.

Tests for Review Lessons may again be ascribed 100 points, with each word or abbreviation counting 2 points. Make sure that pupils understand that they need to write the abbreviations only for the specified words.

The basic goal of Rod and Staff spelling courses is to help pupils master the spelling of the words in the word lists. Therefore, scores from the spelling tests should be given more weight on the final grades than scores from the regular work in the lessons.

Word List

absent 25
acted 7
adore 20
again 7
against 33
all right 14
among 19
angel 16
angry 16
animals 16
another 5
answer 25
aren't 22, 31
arithmetic 19
arrow 2
ashes 4
Ave. 23
awhile 29
balloon 19
basket 25
beach 4
beads 2
beans 2
beautiful 32
because 20
becomes 9
begged 8
beginning 31
believe 32
bench 4
berries 5
Bethlehem 5
Bible 1
bicycle 32
biggest 14
birthday 14
blanket 8
blessing 25
blew 25
blind 1
blood 9
body 2

bother 8
bottle 16
bottom 2
bought 26
bowl 11
boy's 22
branches 4
break 27
breakfast 7
breath 5
bridge 23
bright 11
broke 27
broken 28
brought 20
buckle 16
buggy 2
building 31
built 31
burnt 14
busiest 14
button 9
calves 31
cannot 22
careful 29
carrying 27
cash 4
caught 20
cellar 19
centimeter 31
cents 25
chalkboard 20
changed 23
changing 11
charge 23
chase 25
checks 28
cheer 15
cheese 10
cherry 4
chickens 27
chief 32

children 26
chimney 5
choose 27
chop 4
Christmas 27
churches 4
cities 5
classes 4
clay 10
climbed 11
closed 11
cloth 20
cm 31
coast 11
colors 19
company 19
cookbook 33
cookies 21
copy 1
costs 20
cotton 17
could 21
couldn't 21
counter 22
country 9
cousin 17
covers 9
covet 9
crack 27
cracks 28
create 10
created 11
crossed 25
crowd 22
curl 14
curve 33
Dan. 7
Daniel 7
death 7
deer 15
desert 26
didn't 23

different 19
dirty 16
discolored 28
discover 29
disorderly 28
doctor 8
doesn't 23
dollars 3
downstairs 33
dozen 26
Dr. 8
dressed 7
driver 19
dropped 8
drum 1
dull 3
during 21
earlier 14
early 14
earthworm 14
east 1
easy 26
edge 23
eighteen 17
eighty 17
elephant 31
enemies 20
enemy 19
enjoyed 23
enjoying 22
enough 31
Esth. 7
Esther 7
everywhere 15
evil 16
Ex. 7
Exodus 7
Ezra 7
fairly 15
families 5
farmer's 20
farmers 20

fearful 29
feathers 7
fence 1
few 13
field 3
fields 32
fifteenth 17
fifth 17
finest 13
finished 8
flash 4
flew 13
float 11
flood 31
flour 22
flower 22
follow 3
foot 21
forgave 27
forgotten 27
forty 20
Fri. 10
Friday 10
friend 3
friend's 20
friendly 15
friends 20
fruit 32
ft. 21
fully 21
g 32
gal. 33
gallon 33
Gen. 7
Genesis 7
gentle 16
geography 31
germs 14
giant 23
glory 20
gloves 29
golden 29

good-bye 33
goose 13
grain 1
gram 32
grandfather 15
grandma's 19
grandpa 15
grapes 10
greatest 13, 32
great-
grandmother 33
great-uncle 33
grew 25
ground 22
grown 25
guess 31
hammer 2
handkerchief 31
handle 16
happened 17
haven't 21
health 7
healthy 16
heap 2
heart 15
heathen 5
heaven 7, 31
heavy 10
he'd 25
hello 11
highway 13
holiday 19
hose 26
hour 22
hr. 22
huge 23
hundred 1
hungry 31
hurry 14
I'd 25
idol 16
I'll 23
in. 21
inch 21

instead 7
interesting 19
invite 11
it's 27
jelly 23
joined 22
Josh. 9
Joshua 9
Judg. 9
Judges 9
juice 32
kept 28
kg 32
kilogram 32
kilometer 31
kitchen 4, 27
kitty 2
km 31
l 32
lace 25
ladder 3
language 28
largest 13
later 13, 32
laughed 31
lawn 20
lb. 33
led 26
lessons 17
letters 3
liter 32
loads 3
loaf 3
lock 8
lowest 13
m 31
marbles 16
market 2
match 4
melted 7
Mennonite 19, 33
mercy 25
meter 31
mi. 21

mice 26
middle 16
might 11
mile 21
minister 8
minute 8
Miss 8
mixed 28
mo. 22
Mon. 10
Monday 10
month 22
moonlight 13
mountains 33
mouse 26
mouth 22
Mr. 8
Mrs. 8
muddy 16
mule 13
music 27
myself 1
naughty 20
nearly 15
needle 16
newspaper 14
nineteen 17
ninety 17
noise 26
north 5
Num. 9
Numbers 9
nurse 25
oatmeal 11
ocean 17
o'clock 31
often 17
oldest 14
opened 7
orange 20
oranges 23
ordered 7
others 5
ounce 33

owner 32
oz. 33
package 23
packed 7
pages 11
painting 10, 33
pair 15
papers 2
parents 15
patch 4
peace 10
peaches 4
peas 32
pencil 16
penny 2
person 17
picnic 27
pictures 27, 33
piece 32
pillow 3
pint 33
pitch 4
planned 8
planted 7
plow 22
pocketbook 27
poem 33
points 22
pool 3
porch 4
pound 33
praise 26
prayer 15
preach 10
preacher 19
presents 26
printed 8
Prov. 9
Proverbs 9
pt. 33
pudding 21
pulled 21
pump 1

punish 9
puppy 2
qt. 33
quart 33
question 28
quickly 28
rabbit 2
rainy 16
raise 10
rang 25
rather 5
Rd. 23
reaches 10
ready 1
reasons 26
received 32
recess 25
remember 7
remove 29
ribbon 17
robin 17
rod 2
roots 2
rub 2
rushed 9
sack 1
saddest 14
salvation 29
2 Sam. 9
2 Samuel 9
Sat. 10
Saturday 10
says 9
scare 33
schoolhouse 13
seal 3
seesaw 20
seven 17
seventeen 17
sewing 11
shake 27
shape 4
share 15
sharp 15

shells 4
shining 11, 31
shipped 8
shopping 10
shore 4
should 21
silver 29
since 25
sir 14
sixteen 28
sixty 17
size 26
skates 27
skin 1
sleepy 32
slept 26
slipped 8
slowly 15
smaller 20
smell 3
smooth 13
sofa 3
somewhere 15
sooner 13
soup 1
south 5
space 25
spoil 22
square 28
squirrel 14
St. 23

staff 3
stage 23
station 4
steal 10
steam 1
steel 10
stir 14
stockings 27
stood 21
stories 5, 31
strange 23
straw 20
stream 3
strike 11
studied 11
study 1
suddenly 32
suffer 3
sugar 19
suit 32
Sun. 10
Sunday 10
supply 19
surprise 19
taught 26
teacher's 19
teaches 9
team 2
tear 15
teeth 26
temple 16

term 14
terrible 33
thankful 29
Thanksgiving 28
that's 23
their 15
thick 5
thin 5
thine 5
thinks 9
thinner 14, 32
thirteen 17
thirty 17
thousand 19
threw 13
through 13
throwing 11
Thur. 10
Thursday 10
tiger 2
1 Tim. 9
1 Timothy 9
together 5
tomb 13
tomorrow 33
tooth 13
touch 9
tracks 28
travel 16
tried 11
tries 11

Trinity 19
trouble 9
truly 15
trunk 27
truth 13
Tues. 10
Tuesday 10
tulip 3
tune 13
turkey 5
turtle 16
twelve 29
twice 25
unless 1
unlike 28
unpainted 28
until 1
vacation 29
vegetables 23
violet 32
visited 8, 29
wafers 3
wanted 8
wasn't 22
watched 8, 28
wax 28
wears 15
weather 28
Wed. 10
Wednesday 10
weeds 2

week 22
we're 27
west 1
whenever 29
which 29
whistle 29
whole 5
whose 5
windows 1
wisdom 26
wk. 22
wolf 21
woman 21
women 26
wondered 9, 28
won't 22
wooden 29
wool 21
world 14
wouldn't 21
yard 21
yd. 21
year 22
yoke 29
youngest 29
your 21
you're 21
yourself 29
yr. 22
zone 26

The Weekly Lesson Plan

Part **A, Sounds and Letters,** helps you to hear the sounds in words and helps you to spell those sounds with letters of the alphabet. In this part you will learn to use some patterns that will help you to spell words.

Part **B, Using Your Words,** helps you to learn the meanings of words that we use when we speak and write.

Part **C, Building Words,** helps you to use words and parts of words to build many more words. In this part you will learn to use more patterns that will help you to spell words.

LESSON
1

NEW WORDS

Bible   east
study   west
ready   windows
grain   steam
until   skin
myself   drum
pump   unless
soup   hundred

REVIEW WORDS

sack   copy
blind   fence

A. Sounds and Letters

In the English language, the sounds in words may be spelled with one or more letters. When referring to the sound of a letter or letters, we will place a letter between slashes like this: /a/ for the short **a** sound as in **bat**, or /ā/ for the long **a** sound as in **late**.

Now think about the word **skin** from your spelling list. The /i/ sound is spelled with one letter, **i**. But in **grain**, the /ā/ sound is spelled with the two letters **ai**.

The same sounds may also be spelled with different letters. In the word **skin**, /k/ is spelled **k**. But in **copy**, /k/ is spelled **c**.

Write the spelling words that have these sounds.

1. /ē/ /s/ /t/ _____ east _____

2. /f/ /e/ /n/ /s/ _____ fence _____

3. /s/ /a/ /k/ _____ sack _____

4. /d/ /r/ /u/ /m/ _____ drum _____

5. /s/ /t/ /ē/ /m/ _____ steam _____

6. /r/ /e/ /d/ /ē/ _____ ready _____

7. /m/ /ī/ /s/ /e/ /l/ /f/ _____ myself _____

Dictionaries usually show the pronunciation of words with phonetic spellings like this: **kāk** for **cake**.

Write spelling words for these phonetic spellings.

8. kop'ē _____ copy _____

9. stud'ē _____ study _____

10. win'dōz _____ windows _____

11. sōōp _____ soup _____

12. grān _____ grain _____

13. un les' _____ unless _____

14. hun'drid _____ hundred _____

A. 28 points

4

Test Sentences

(Teacher: To give spelling tests, pronounce each spelling word, read the sentence, and pronounce the word again.)

1. *soup*   On a cold day, hot *soup* tastes good.
2. *grain*   Jesus' disciples picked *grain* to eat.
3. *west*   Grandfather lives a mile *west* of us.
4. *pump*   Do you have a *pump* on your farm?
5. *east*   The wise men saw a star in the *east*.
6. *study*   We should *study* to do our own business.
7. *hundred*   One *hundred* is less than one thousand.
8. *drum*   A large *drum* can be used to store feed.
9. *skin*   Did you ever *skin* a rabbit?
10. *windows* We washed the *windows* on Saturday.
11. *until*   Everyone slept *until* morning.

15. From each pair below, copy the word that has a short vowel sound.

/a/   **sack   trade** _____sack_____

/e/   **steam   west** _____west_____

/i/   **Bible   skin** _____skin_____

/o/   **copy   load** _____copy_____

/u/   **cube   study** _____study_____

16. From each pair below, copy the word that has a long vowel sound.

/ā/   **last   grain** _____grain_____

/ē/   **east   send** _____east_____

/ī/   **still   blind** _____blind_____

/ō/   **stop   hold** _____hold_____

/yo͞o/   **use   must** _____use_____

Write the answers.

17. Which NEW WORD

a. begins with /ē/? _____east_____

b. has both /t/ and /l/? _____until_____

18. Which NEW WORD begins and ends with the same consonant? _____pump_____

19. Which REVIEW WORD has /e/? __fence__

B. Using Your Words

Fill in the blanks with spelling words from the first column.

The early Americans soon discovered that corn was a very important

(1) _____grain_____. They did not know how to plant or grow it **(2)** _____until_____ the Indians showed them how. At nearly every meal, the pioneers ate corn in some form. Sometimes they cooked it and used it in **(3)** _____soup_____. For a special treat, they roasted the ear of corn until it was **(4)** _____ready_____ to eat. The colonists used corn for money. Would it not seem strange to give corn instead of money for a **(5)** _____Bible_____ to read?

Some words have more than one meaning. Write the same spelling word in both sentences of each set.

6. The _____steam_____ from the boiling water made the room feel damp.

A cup of hot tea will _____steam_____.

7. "And that ye _____study_____ to be quiet, and to do your own business."

Father went into his _____study_____ to write a letter.

B. 27 points

Answers may be NEW WORDS or REVIEW WORDS.

5

---

12. *Bible*   The *Bible* is the Word of God.
13. *ready*   Ruth was *ready* to gather grain for Naomi.
14. *myself*   I can read the Bible *myself*.
15. *unless*   We shall go outside *unless* it rains.
16. *steam*   Water turns to *steam* when it boils.

Now for the REVIEW WORDS, instead of writing only the words, you will write the sentences. Let's try one sentence. You listen carefully. I will say the sentence once, and then a second time. Wait to write until I have said the sentence twice. Then you write the entire sentence. Begin the sentence with a capital letter and end it with a period. Here is the sentence. Listen while I say it twice.

The *blind* girl did not see the *fence*.

Now we have one more sentence. Wait to write until I say the sentence twice. Then write the entire sentence. Remember to begin with a capital letter and end with a period.

Copy the name on the *sack*.

8. In Bible times, bottles of ____skin____ were made from hides of small animals.

Be careful not to ____skin____ your knee.

9. Pull the ____blind____ at the window to keep out the bright sunshine.

Fanny Crosby was ____blind____, yet her songs often speak of seeing.

10. Scribes worked many hours to ____copy____ the whole Bible.

A ____copy____ of the Bible was once hidden in a loaf of bread.

Answer these questions.

11. Which spelling word

a. is a number? ____hundred____

b. names a prepared food? ____soup____

12. Which two NEW WORDS name directions?

____east____   ____west____

13. Write the second column of NEW WORDS in alphabetical order. For words beginning with the same letter, you must look at the second letter to place them correctly.

____drum____

____east____

____hundred____

____skin____

____steam____

____unless____

____west____

____windows____

C. Building Words

but ton hole   won der

1. Say these words slowly. Hear the syllables.

One syllable:

but   won   scratch

Two syllables:

but ton   won der   scrib ble

Three syllables:

but ton hole   won der ful   shoe mak er

2. Circle the one vowel in each word.

an   bell   truck

3. A word with only one vowel sound has how many syllables? ____one____

4. Circle the two vowels in each word.

begin   holding   wagon

5. A word with two vowel sounds has how many syllables? ____two____

6. Underline the words that have two syllables.

west	myself	skin
windows	dind	pump
Bible	study	hundred

C. 31 points

6

7. The word **steam** has two vowels but only one vowel sound. What is that vowel sound? __/ē/ (long e)__

8. Write four other spelling words in which two vowels together make one vowel sound.

__ready__   __grain__

__soup__   __east__

9. In which three NEW WORDS do you hear /un/ in the first syllable?   __until__

__unless__   __hundred__

10. How many syllables does each word in number 9 have?   __two__

11. Which NEW WORD ends with **s** because it names more than one?   __windows__

12. Which REVIEW WORD has two syllables?

__copy__

13. Which NEW WORD begins with a capital letter because it names a particular book?

__Bible__

14. Which NEW WORD contains the word **self**?

__myself__

Bible Thoughts

Use a spelling word to complete this sentence.

15. The __Bible__ is the Word of God.

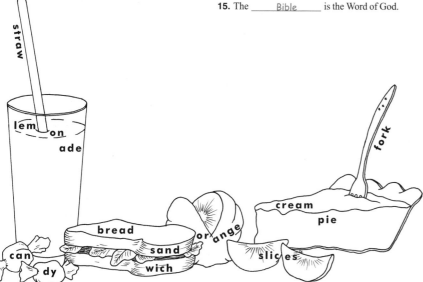

"We thank Thee, Lord, for this our food."

7

LESSON 2

NEW WORDS

bottom   beads
rabbit   kitty
body   heap
team   hammer
arrow   roots
beans   rod
market   buggy
papers   weeds

REVIEW WORDS

penny   rub
tiger   puppy

p/ā/**p**ers

p/e/**pp**ers

3. Write the NEW WORD that begins with a vowel sound. _____arrow_____

A. Sounds and Letters

> • At the beginning or end of a word, a consonant sound is usually spelled with a single letter.

1. Write the spelling words that begin with /b/.

bottom	beans
body	beads
buggy	

2. Write a REVIEW WORD that ends with /b/.

_____rub_____

> • Between two vowel sounds, a consonant sound is usually spelled with a single letter when the vowel sound before it is long. **me**t**er**
> When the first vowel sound is short, the consonant sound is usually spelled with double letters. **mi**tt**en**

4. Write a NEW WORD and a REVIEW WORD that have a long vowel followed by a single consonant.

_____papers_____   _____tiger_____

5. Write eight spelling words that have a short vowel followed by a double consonant.

bottom	hammer
rabbit	buggy
arrow	penny
kitty	puppy

6. Which NEW WORD has /ē/ spelled **ee**?

_____weeds_____

A. 23 points

8

Test Sentences

1.	*hammer*	God's Word is like a *hammer*.
2.	*weeds*	We pulled *weeds* in the garden.
3.	*kitty*	Treat the *kitty* kindly.
4.	*beads*	When the string tore, the *beads* scattered.
5.	*market*	In Bible times, children played in the *market*.
6.	*bottom*	The *bottom* of the bucket is rusty.
7.	*rod*	Moses held his *rod* over the Red Sea.
8.	*heap*	Mother gave me a *heap* of mashed potatoes.
9.	*papers*	Keep these *papers* in your notebook.
10.	*rabbit*	My pet *rabbit* eats lettuce.
11.	*arrow*	Jonathan shot an *arrow* beyond the lad.
12.	*buggy*	A horse and *buggy* passed our house.

Write spelling words for these phonetic spellings.

7. bēnz ___beans___

8. hēp ___heap___

9. mär′kit ___market___

10. tēm ___team___

11. ham′ər ___hammer___

B. Using Your Words

B. 39 points

Fill in the blanks with spelling words from the first column.

One of the marvelous works that God has made is an extraordinary bean called a jumping bean. Each of these **(1)** ___beans___ has a caterpillar living inside. When the caterpillar moves its **(2)** ___body___ , it moves the bean as well. It may move its bean house several inches at a time as it moves around the **(3)** ___bottom___ of a container. These beans are not to be eaten but may be sold as novelties at a **(4)** ___market___ . Would you spend a **(5)** ___penny___ for one of these unusual beans?

6. Write two sentences of your own. Use **rabbit** and **kitty** in the first sentence. Use **tiger** and **puppy** in the second sentence.

6. Allow 2 points per sentence.

a. ___(Individual sentences. Pupils may change the specified words to a___

b. ___different number or tense, but the form must be spelled correctly.)___

Write the spelling word that belongs with each group.

7. corn, peas, carrots ___beans___

8. dime, nickel, quarter ___penny___

9. screwdriver, saw, pliers ___hammer___

10. pencil, eraser, books ___papers___

11. wagon, sleigh, cart ___buggy___

12. lion, zebra, elephant ___tiger___

13. bow, arrowhead, target ___arrow___

14. stick, pole, bar ___rod___

15. polish, scour, scrub ___rub___

16. leaves, branches, trunk ___roots___

Write the spelling word that each phrase makes you think of.

17. A place to buy things. ___market___

18. Unwanted plants. ___weeds___

19. A pile. ___heap___

20. Opposite of **top**. ___bottom___

9

13. *roots*   Tiny hairs on tree *roots* drink in water.
14. *team*   Grandfather plowed with a *team* of horses.
15. *beans*   Green *beans* give us many vitamins.
16. *body*   All parts of the *body* work together.

Now for the REVIEW WORDS, instead of only writing the words, you will write the sentences. Listen carefully. I will say a sentence two times. Wait to write until I have said the sentence two times. Then write the entire sentence. Begin it with a capital letter and end it with a period. Here is the sentence.

A *tiger* can *rub* his head.

Here is the next sentence. Wait to write until I say the sentence twice. Remember to begin with a capital letter and end with a period.

My *puppy* sees a *penny*.

Write the same spelling word in both sentences of each set.

21. Please ___hammer___ the nail carefully.

Then put the ___hammer___ away.

22. The ___roots___ of a tree go deep into the ground.

A hog often ___roots___ in the dirt.

23. Give this string of ___beads___ to your baby sister.

Father wiped ___beads___ of sweat from his forehead.

Write each group of words in alphabetical order.

24. bottom ___arrow___

arrow ___bottom___

heap ___heap___

team ___rabbit___

rabbit ___team___

25. market ___drum___

penny ___kitty___

kitty ___market___

weeds ___penny___

drum ___weeds___

C. Building Words

Write these words, saying them slowly in syllables. Write the number of syllables after each word.

1. papers ___papers___ 2

2. market ___market___ 2

3. rub ___rub___ 1

4. tiger ___tiger___ 2

5. rabbit ___rabbit___ 2

6. roots ___roots___ 1

- **Syllables**
  A word with two consonants between two vowels is divided into syllables between the two consonants. This is the VC/CV pattern, for vowel-consonant-consonant-vowel.

  VC CV   VC CV
  les/son   win/dow

Write VCCV above four letters in each of the following words. Then draw a slash to divide the syllables.

V C C V   V C C V
7. h a m/m e r   k i t/t y

V C C V   V C C V
8. p e n/n y   r a b/b i t

V C C V   V C C V
9. m a r/k e t   u n/l e s s

Write these words. Use slashes to divide the syllables.

10. buggy ___bug/gy___

11. puppy ___pup/py___

C. 49 points

12. bottom   _____bot/tom_____

13. unless   _____un/less_____

14. summer   _____sum/mer_____

15. arrow   _____ar/row_____

16. until   _____un/til_____

• **Singular and Plural Nouns**
   A singular noun names one
   person, place, or thing.
   friend   school   story
   A plural noun names more than
   one person, place, or thing.
   friends   schools   stories

---

17. All the NEW WORDS in this lesson are nouns.
   Write the NEW WORDS that are singular
   nouns.

bottom	_kitty_
rabbit	_heap_
body	_hammer_
team	_rod_
arrow	_buggy_
market	

18. Write the NEW WORDS that are plural nouns.

beans	_roots_
papers	_weeds_
beads	

19. The plural forms of most nouns are made
   by adding -s. Write the plurals of the words
   below.

arrow _____arrows_____

hammer _____hammers_____

rabbit _____rabbits_____

market _____markets_____

20. Write the REVIEW WORDS that are singular
   nouns with two syllables.   _____penny_____
   _____tiger_____   _____puppy_____

Bible Thoughts

**Use a spelling word to
complete this Bible verse.**

21. "Thy _____rod_____ and thy staff they
   comfort me" (Psalm 23:4).

11

LESSON 3

NEW WORDS

follow
loads
tulip
pool
stream
dollars
smell
field

letters
staff
sofa
friend
wafers
suffer
ladder
seal

REVIEW WORDS

dull
loaf

pillow
puff

A. Sounds and Letters

• When /f/ or /l/ is at the end of a one-syllable word and follows a short vowel sound, /f/ or /l/ is usually spelled **ff** or **ll**.
  cli_ff_   **we_ll_**

1. Write four spelling words that follow the rule above.

smell   dull

staff   puff

2. Now write a one-syllable spelling word having the /ō/ sound and ending with /f/, and a one-syllable spelling word having the /ē/ sound and ending with /l/.

loaf   seal

3. Write six two-syllable spelling words that that have a double consonant after a short vowel sound.

follow   suffer

dollars   ladder

letters   pillow

4. Now write three two-syllable spelling words that have a single consonant after a long vowel sound.

tulip   wafers

sofa

Write a spelling word for each phonetic spelling.

5. lōdz — loads

6. strēm — stream

7. fēld — field

8. frend — friend

9. sēl — seal

10. dol'ərz — dollars

A. 32 points

12

Test Sentences

1. *smell* — Did you *smell* the smoke?
2. *sofa* — Father bought a *sofa* for our living room.
3. *pool* — The blind man washed in the *pool* of Siloam.
4. *ladder* — Jacob saw a *ladder* reaching to heaven.
5. *follow* — Christians *follow* Christ.
6. *suffer* — Jesus had to *suffer* much pain.
7. *seal* — We *seal* our letters before we mail them.
8. *field* — Ruth gleaned in a *field* of barley.
9. *stream* — A *stream* flows through our pasture.
10. *dollars* — Two *dollars* equal forty nickels.
11. *letters* — Write *letters* to your grandparents.
12. *loads* — Father *loads* the wagon with wood.

11. Write one NEW WORD that begins with the /p/ sound and one that ends with the /p/ sound.

_____pool_____   _____tulip_____

12. Two or three consonants that blend their sounds together are called a **consonant blend**. Three consonant blends are **st**, **str**, and **mp**. Write the NEW WORDS that begin with consonant blends.

_____stream_____   _____staff_____

_____smell_____   _____friend_____

13. Write the NEW WORDS that end with consonant blends.

_____field_____   _____friend_____

14. In which NEW WORD does **ie** spell /e/?

_____friend_____

15. In which NEW WORD does **ie** spell /ē/?

_____field_____

16. Write the NEW WORD that has /ər/ spelled **ar**.

_____dollars_____

B. 32 points

B. Using Your Words

Fill in the blanks with spelling words from the first column.

Jesus said, "Consider the lilies of the **(1)** _____field_____ ." We are to take time

to think about these lovely flowers with their fragrant **(2)** _____smell_____ and their

bright or **(3)** _____dull_____ colors. Solomon may have spent hundreds of

(4) _____dollars_____ for his clothes, but Jesus said they were not as beautiful as the

lilies. Since God made such beautiful flowers and takes cares of them, He will take care

of us too. He wants us to trust and **(5)** _____follow_____ Him always. His Word is like

a **(6)** _____stream_____ of living water flowing through a desert.

7. Write two sentences of your own. In the first sentence use the words **dollars** and **loaf**. In the second sentence use **tulip** and **friend**.

a. _____(Individual sentences.)_____

b. _____

13

13. *wafers*   Mother gave us vanilla *wafers* for lunch.
14. *staff*   The shepherd carried a *staff* and a rod.
15. *tulip*   Jane picked a purple *tulip* in the garden.
16. *friend*   We love a *friend* in spite of his faults.

Listen while I say a sentence two times. Then write the sentence.

She made her *pillow puff* up.

Here is the next sentence.

This is too *dull* to cut a *loaf* of bread.

Write the spelling word that belongs with each group.

8. violet, pansy, rose _____tulip_____

9. biscuits, crackers, cookies ____wafers____

10. chair, table, bed _____sofa_____

11. brook, river, creek _____stream_____

Complete each sentence with a spelling word that means the same as the boldface word.

12. **stick**   Jacob worshiped, leaning upon the top of his _____staff_____.

13. **companion**   Abraham was called the _____friend_____ of God.

14. **small pond**   The blind man washed in the _____pool_____ of Siloam.

15. **written messages**   While Paul was in prison, he wrote _____letters_____ to the churches.

16. **stamp**   Mordecai used the king's ring to _____seal_____ the letters.

17. **allow**   God will not _____suffer_____ the foot of the righteous to be moved (Psalm 121:3).

18. **something used to climb**   In Jacob's dream, he saw a _____ladder_____ reaching from earth to heaven.

19. **bread baked in one piece**   The disciples had not more than one _____loaf_____ of bread on the ship.

Write the spelling word that each phrase makes you think of.

20. Beautiful flower. _____tulip_____

21. Place to plant corn. _____field_____

22. Not sharp. _____dull_____

23. Go after. _____follow_____

24. Small cookies. _____wafers_____

25. Write the spelling words below in alphabetical order. Since the first letters are alike, you must look at the second letter in each word.

smell	_____seal_____
staff	_____smell_____
sofa	_____sofa_____
suffer	_____staff_____
seal	_____suffer_____

C. Building Words

C. 13 points

• **Syllables**

If a word has one consonant between two vowels, it is divided after the consonant if the first vowel is short: VC/V.   **met/al**
If the first vowel is long, the word is divided after the first vowel: V/CV.   **me/ter**

1. Write **copy** and **robin**. Use slashes to divide the syllables.

cop/y   rob/in

2. Write **sofa** and **wafers**. Use slashes to divide the syllables.

so/fa   wa/fers

• A syllable containing a short vowel sound usually ends with a consonant. A syllable containing a long vowel sound usually ends with that long vowel sound.

3. Write **dollar** and **study**. Use slashes to divide the syllables.

dol/lar   stud/y

4. Write **tiger** and **Bible**. Use slashes to divide the syllables.

ti/ger   Bi/ble

5. To make most nouns plural, we add **s** to the noun. Write four NEW WORDS that are plural nouns.

loads   letters

dollars   wafers

Bible Thoughts

Use the plural form of a REVIEW WORD to complete this verse.

6. "There is a lad here, which hath five barley

loaves   , and two small

fishes: but what are they among so many?"

(John 6:9).

Lesson 4—91 points

LESSON 4

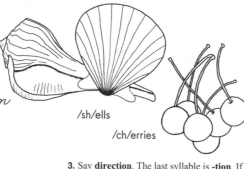

/sh/ells

/ch/erries

NEW WORDS

cherry
branches
shape
peaches
churches
match
classes
chop

kitchen
shells
bench
patch
cash
flash
pitch
station

REVIEW WORDS

porch
shore

beach
ashes

A. Sounds and Letters

- Two letters that spell one sound are called a digraph. The /sh/ sound is usually spelled with the digraph **sh**. **sha__p__e** **fla__sh__**

1. Write the spelling words that

   a. begin with /sh/. ___shape___

   ___shells___   ___shore___

   b. end with /sh/. ___cash___

   ___flash___

2. Which word ended with /sh/ before **-es** was added? ___ashes___

3. Say **direction**. The last syllable is **-tion**. If **o** spells the vowel sound in **-tion**, what two letters spell the /sh/ sound? ___ti___

   Write the NEW WORD in which /sh/ is spelled

   ti. ___station___

- The /ch/ sound is most often spelled **ch**. **cherry** **bench** After a short vowel sound, /ch/ is usually spelled **tch**. **ma__tch__** **ki__tch__en**

4. Write the spelling words in which /ch/ is spelled **tch** after a short vowel sound.

   ___match___   ___patch___

   ___kitchen___   ___pitch___

5. Write the spelling words in which /ch/ is spelled **ch** (not **tch**).

   ___cherry___   ___chop___

   ___branches___   ___bench___

   ___peaches___   ___porch___

   ___churches___   ___beach___

6. In which NEW WORD does the root word begin and end with /ch/? ___churches___

A. 38 points

16

Test Sentences

1. *kitchen*   Our *kitchen* is a busy place.
2. *shells*   Jerry gathered *shells* of all sizes.
3. *flash*   What a big *flash* of lightning!
4. *classes*   We have two *classes* before recess.
5. *churches*   John Nolt preached at two *churches* on Sunday.
6. *match*   To light a *match,* use great care.
7. *peaches*   Ripe *peaches* contain vitamin C.
8. *pitch*   The ark was covered with *pitch,* or tar.
9. *cherry*   Mother made a delicious *cherry* cobbler.
10. *branches*   Those *branches* are loaded with fruit.
11. *bench*   We sat on the third *bench* at the meeting.
12. *patch*   My coat has a *patch* on it.

7. Which spelling words begin with the consonant blends **fl**, **cl**, **st**, or **br**?

_____flash_____   _____station_____

_____classes_____   _____branches_____

Write spelling words for these phonetic spellings.

8. shāp _____shape_____

9. stā′shən _____station_____

10. bēch _____beach_____

11. kich′ən _____kitchen_____

12. cher′ē _____cherry_____

13. a. Write the NEW WORD that has /l/ spelled

ll. _____shells_____

b. Does a short or long vowel sound come

before the **ll**? _____short_____

14. Write **match**. Then write three other words by changing the first letter to **c**, **h**, and **l**.

_____match_____   _____hatch_____

_____catch_____   _____latch_____

15. Which spelling words end with **e**?

_____shape_____   _____shore_____

B. 32 points

B. Using Your Words

Fill in the blanks with spelling words from the first column.

Prune means "to cut or **(1)** _____chop_____ out useless parts." When a tree is pruned, only the main and necessary **(2)** _____branches_____ remain. Peach trees are pruned so that they bear better **(3)** _____peaches_____. Other fruit trees, such as apple and **(4)** _____cherry_____ trees, are also pruned. The top of a shade tree should not be pruned because then the **(5)** _____shape_____ of the tree is spoiled. Just as pruning is important for trees, it is important in our lives too. We need to cut away bad habits like unkindness, selfishness, lying, and cheating.

6. Write two sentences of your own. Use **shape** and **shells** in the first sentence. Use **kitchen** and **bench** in the second sentence.

a. _____(Individual sentences.)_____

b. _____

17

13. *shape*   The cloud had the *shape* of a camel.
14. *cash*   Judas carried the disciples' *cash* in a bag.
15. *chop*   Our neighbors *chop* wood every Saturday.
16. *station*   We stopped at a gas *station* for gas.

Sweep the *ashes* off the *porch*.

A *beach* is a flat *shore*.

7. Words that have nearly the same meaning
are called **synonyms**. Match the synonyms
by placing the letters in column B before
the correct words in column A.

A	B
_d_ beach	a. throw
_e_ shape	b. money
_g_ classes	c. seat
_a_ pitch	d. shore
_c_ bench	e. form
_f_ patch	f. mend
_b_ cash	g. groups

**Use the synonyms in column A above to
complete the following sentences.**

8. Catch the ball when I _____pitch_____ it.

9. Mother will need to _____patch_____ the
torn shirt.

10. Noah took two _____classes_____ of animals,
clean and unclean, into the ark.

11. When paying by mail, it is safer to send
checks than _____cash_____ .

12. This animal cracker is in the _____shape_____
of a giraffe.

13. In church Regina kneels in front of the
_____bench_____ to pray.

14. Write these spelling words in alphabetical
order. With some words you may need to
look at the third letter to see which word
comes first.

shore	cherry
cherry	churches
shells	shape
churches	shells
station	shore
shape	station

**Write the same spelling word in both
sentences of each set.**

15. Paul tried to _____shape_____ the clay so
that it looked like a horse.

The Holy Spirit came upon Jesus in the
_____shape_____ of a dove.

16. We saw some pretty shells lying on the
_____beach_____ .

The men hoped to _____beach_____ the
rowboat without damaging it.

C. Building Words

> • **Plural Nouns**
>   When a plural noun is formed by adding **es**, pronounced /iz/, another syllable is added to the root word.

1. Write the plural spelling words that end with /iz/.

branches	classes
peaches	ashes
churches	

2. How many syllables are in each word that you wrote for number 1? ____two____

3. Write the plural forms of these spelling words. Use slashes to divide the words into syllables.

match _____-____ match/es _____
porch _____ porch/es _____
bench _____ bench/es _____
patch _____ patch/es _____
flash _____ flash/es _____
pitch _____ pitch/es _____
beach _____ beach/es _____

Dictionary Practice

4. The words that you look up in a dictionary are called **entry words**. They are in boldface and are listed in alphabetical order along with information about them. An entry word and the information about it is called an **entry**. A meaning that a dictionary gives for a word is called a **definition**.

a. In the Speller Dictionary, what is the first entry word that starts with **s**?

_____sack_____

b. What is the definition of this word?

___A large bag made of coarse cloth.___

_____

5. How many entries does the Speller Dictionary have for each letter below?

K ___7___   V ___4___

Q ___4___   Z ___1___

Bible Thoughts

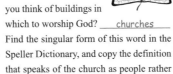

6. Which NEW WORD makes you think of buildings in which to worship God? ___churches___ Find the singular form of this word in the Speller Dictionary, and copy the definition that speaks of the church as people rather than a building.

_____Group of people with_____

_____the same religious beliefs_____

LESSON 5

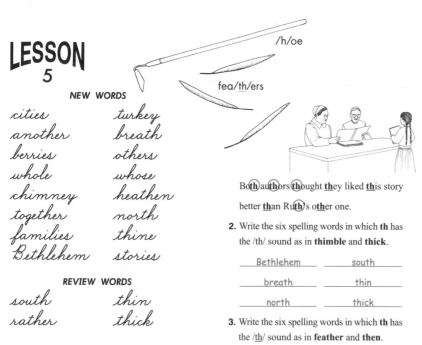

/h/oe

fea/<u>th</u>/ers

NEW WORDS

cities	turkey
another	breath
berries	others
whole	whose
chimney	heathen
together	north
families	thine
Bethlehem	stories

REVIEW WORDS

south	thin
rather	thick

A. Sounds and Letters

> • The consonant sound /th/ as in **thimble** and /<u>th</u>/ as in **feather** are both spelled with the digraph **th**. You blow through your teeth to make the /th/ sound in **thimble** and **thick**. You use your voice to make the /<u>th</u>/ sound in **feather** and **then**.

1. In the following sentence, say each word carefully to yourself. Then draw a circle around the **th** in each word that has the /th/ sound. Draw one line under the **th** in each word that has the /<u>th</u>/ sound.

Both authors thought they liked this story better than Ruth's other one.

2. Write the six spelling words in which **th** has the /th/ sound as in **thimble** and **thick**.

Bethlehem	south
breath	thin
north	thick

3. Write the six spelling words in which **th** has the /<u>th</u>/ sound as in **feather** and **then**.

another	heathen
together	thine
others	rather

> • The /h/ sound is usually spelled with the letter **h** as in **his**. At the beginning of a few words, /h/ is spelled **wh** as in **whose**.

4. Which spelling words begin with /h/?

whole	heathen
whose	

5. Which NEW WORD has /h/ at the beginning of the last syllable? _Bethlehem_

A. 35 points

20

Test Sentences

1.	*stories*	Jesus told many *stories* called parables.
2.	*another*	God gave Jacob *another* name.
3.	*breath*	We were glad for a *breath* of fresh air.
4.	*whose*	A woman *whose* son had died came to Jesus.
5.	*chimney*	The *chimney* is made of brick.
6.	*north*	A dairy farm is *north* of our house.
7.	*together*	Christians meet *together* for worship.
8.	*Bethlehem*	To *Bethlehem* the shepherds hurried.
9.	*heathen*	The *heathen* people do not know Jesus.
10.	*cities*	Several large *cities* are in our state.
11.	*others*	We try to treat *others* kindly.
12.	*whole*	Mother canned *whole* tomatoes.

6. Write **heathen**. _____heathen_____

What two vowels spell /ē/? _____ea_____

7. Which NEW WORD begins with /ch/?

_____chimney_____ How is /ch/ spelled? _ch_

8. Which spelling word has a double conso-

nant? _____berries_____

9. Which spelling word begins with /s/

spelled **c**? _____cities_____

10. Which spelling word ends with /k/ spelled

ck? _____thick_____

Write spelling words for these phonetic spellings.

11. tûr′kē _____turkey_____

12. ber′ēz _____berries_____

13. fam′ə lēz _____families_____

14. stôr′ēz _____stories_____

B. Using Your Words

B. 26 points

Fill in the blanks with spelling words from the first column.

We know that blueberries and cranberries are **(1)** _____berries_____ , but so are bananas.

There is **(2)** _____another_____ interesting thing about the banana. It grows on a treelike

plant that is not a tree. When bananas are to be shipped to faraway **(3)** _____cities_____ ,

the **(4)** _____whole_____ bunch is picked green and allowed to ripen on its way to the

market. Bananas in their dirtproof and germproof peelings are a fruit that many

(5) _____families_____ enjoy eating.

6. Write two sentences of your own. Use **Bethlehem** and **stories** in the first sentence. Use **turkey**
and **berries** in the second sentence.

a. _____(Individual sentences.)_____

b. _____

Write the spelling words that have these meanings.

7. Person who does not believe in God.

_____heathen_____

8. Belonging to thee. _____thine_____

9. City in Judea where Jesus was born.

_____Bethlehem_____

10. Not thick. _____thin_____

11. More willingly. _____rather_____

12. With each other. _____together_____

21

13. *turkey*   The wild *turkey* lives in the mountains.
14. *families*   People in *families* help each other.
15. *thine* (or *Thine*)   I am *Thine* for service, Lord.
16. *berries*   The *berries* will ripen in June.

Look *south rather* than west.

The soup may be *thick* or *thin*.

13. Air drawn into and forced out of the lungs.

_____breath_____

14. Different persons or things. ___others___

15. Belonging to whom. ___whose___

16. Not thin. ___thick___

17. Words that are pronounced alike but have different meanings are called **homophones**. Use **whole** and **hole** in these sentences.

a. The rabbit quickly dashed into its

___hole___.

b. Mother, will you please mend this

___hole___ in my shirt?

c. God fed the ___whole___ camp of Israel with manna.

d. Our family ate a ___whole___ water-melon.

18. Which NEW WORD and REVIEW WORD name opposite directions?

___north___   ___south___

19. What word do we use today instead of **thine**? ___yours___

The term *homonyms* has been replaced by *homophones* in current usage.

C. Building Words

• **Plural Nouns**
To form the plural of a noun that ends with **y** preceded by a consonant, change the **y** to **i** and add **-es**.
    story—stories   city—cities

1. Write the plural forms of the underlined nouns by changing **y** to **i** and adding **-es**.

a. One <u>berry</u> costs one <u>penny</u>. Five

___berries___ cost five ___pennies___.

b. This <u>story</u> is about a <u>pony</u>. These

___stories___ are about ___ponies___.

c. In this <u>country</u> you can see a blue <u>sky</u>. In

many ___countries___ you can see blue

___skies___.

2. Write the plural forms of these nouns.
copy   puppy   body   buggy

___copies___   ___bodies___

___puppies___   ___buggies___

• **To form the plural of a noun that ends with y preceded by a vowel, add only -s to the singular form.**
    ray—rays   pulley—pulleys

3. Write the plural forms of the underlined words by simply adding **-s**.

a. Give the <u>key</u> to the <u>boy</u>. Give the

___keys___ to the ___boys___.

b. Pedro led the <u>donkey</u> down the <u>alley</u>.

Pedro led the ___donkeys___ down the

___alleys___.

C. 30 points

c. I ate my lunch on a <u>tray</u> one <u>day</u>. We ate
our lunches on ____trays____ some
____days____ .

4. Write the plural forms of these nouns.
toy   valley   turkey   chimney

____toys____	____turkeys____
____valleys____	____chimneys____

Dictionary Practice

5. For each letter, copy the first entry word in
the Speller Dictionary.

H ____hammer____   P ____pack____

M ____marble____   W ____wafer____

6. Often a dictionary gives more than one definition for an entry word. For each underlined word below, copy the correct definition
from the Speller Dictionary.

a. I like the <u>smell</u> of lilacs.

_____Odor._____

b. We met Grandpa at the train <u>station</u>.

____Regular stopping place.____

c. Be sure to <u>study</u> your memory verse.

_____Try to learn._____

d. Jesus said, "<u>Suffer</u> the little children to
come unto me."

_____Allow; permit._____

Bible Thoughts

Use spelling words to
complete these Bible verses.

7. "By the word of the LORD were the heav-
ens made; and all the host of them by the
____breath____ of his mouth" (Psalm 33:6).

8. "Why do the ____heathen____ rage, and the
people imagine a vain thing?" (Psalm 2:1)

23

34   Grade 4 Spelling

LESSON 6

1	2	3	4	5
Bible	bottom	follow	cherry	cities
study	rabbit	loads	branches	another
ready	body	tulip	shape	berries
grain	team	pool	peaches	whole
until	arrow	stream	churches	chimney
myself	beans	dollars	match	together
pump	market	smell	classes	families
soup	papers	field	chop	Bethlehem
east	beads	letters	kitchen	turkey
west	kitty	staff	shells	breath
windows	heap	sofa	bench	others
steam	hammer	friend	patch	whose
skin	roots	wafers	cash	heathen
drum	rod	suffer	flash	north
unless	buggy	ladder	pitch	thine
hundred	weeds	seal	station	stories

A. Sounds and Letters Review

A. 59 points

1. Write the words below. Be sure to spell each initial consonant sound correctly.

   /b/uggy _____buggy_____

   /t/ogether _____together_____

2. In number 1 above, you spelled each initial consonant sound by using a (<u>single</u>, double) letter. (Underline the answer.)

3. Write the words below. Be sure to use the correct consonants.

   pa/p/ers _____papers_____

   wa/f/ers _____wafers_____

4. In number 3 above, the first vowel sound in each word is long. So you used a (<u>single</u>, double) letter to spell the consonant sound after that vowel.

5. Write the words below. Be sure to use the correct consonants.

   la/d/er _____ladder_____

   bo/t/om _____bottom_____

6. In number 5 above, the first vowel sound in each word is short. So you used a (single, <u>double</u>) letter to spell the consonant sound after that vowel.

7. Write **study**, **body**, and **city**. ___study___

   ___body___   ___city___

24

Review—Test Sentences

1. *west*   The sun sets in the *west* each evening.
2. *body*   An ocean is a large *body* of water.
3. *north*   Wind from the *north* is cold.
4. *letters* Paul wrote *letters*, called epistles, to the churches.
5. *skin*   Gehazi saw that his *skin* was white.
6. *another* The widow asked for *another* vessel.
7. *pool*   Jesus sent the blind man to a *pool* to wash.
8. *pump*   The plumber fixed the *pump* in the barn.
9. *cash*   She pays *cash* for groceries.
10. *friend* "A *friend* loveth at all times."
11. *papers* A pile of *papers* blew off the desk.
12. *beans*   We ate green *beans* and potatoes.

8. In number 7 above, the first vowel sound in each word is (<u>short</u>, long). But the consonants after them are spelled with (<u>single</u>, double) letters.

9. Write the words below. Be sure to spell each final consonant sound correctly.

   dru/m/ <u>drum</u>   sou/p/ <u>soup</u>

10. You spelled each final consonant sound in number 9 with a (<u>single</u>, double) letter.

11. Write these words that end with /f/ and /l/.

    sea/l/ <u>seal</u>   sta/f/ <u>staff</u>

    sme/l/ <u>smell</u>   loa/f/ <u>loaf</u>

12. In number 11 above, you used a (<u>single</u>, double) consonant to spell /f/ or /l/ after a long vowel sound. You used a (single, <u>double</u>) consonant to spell /f/ or /l/ after a short vowel sound.

13. Change the underlined consonants to /ch/. Write the words you make.

    to<u>p</u> <u>chop</u>   ma<u>p</u> <u>match</u>

    ben<u>d</u> <u>bench</u>   pi<u>n</u> <u>pitch</u>

    pea<u>k</u> <u>peach</u>   bur<u>n</u> <u>church</u>

14. In number 13 above, you used (ch, <u>tch</u>) to spell /ch/ after a short vowel sound. You used (<u>ch</u>, tch) to spell /ch/ at other places.

15. Change the underlined consonants to /sh/. Write the words you make.

    ca<u>t</u> <u>cash</u>   be<u>lls</u> <u>shells</u>

    fla<u>g</u> <u>flash</u>   ca<u>pe</u> <u>shape</u>

16. In number 15, you used the letters <u>sh</u> to spell every /sh/ sound.

17. In which Lesson 4 word is /sh/ spelled **ti**?

    <u>station</u>

18. The /th/ and /<u>th</u>/ sounds are usually spelled <u>th</u>.

19. Change the underlined consonants to /th/.

    brea<u>d</u> <u>breath</u>   si<u>ck</u> <u>thick</u>

20. Change the underlined consonants to /<u>th</u>/.

    <u>m</u>ine <u>thine</u>   <u>h</u>en <u>then</u>

21. Which of the Lesson 5 words begin with /h/?

    <u>whole ✓</u>   <u>whose ✓</u>

    <u>heathen</u>

22. In number 21 above, put a check mark (✓) after each word that has /h/ spelled **wh**.

23. Which Lesson 1 words have the consonant blends **mp**, **gr**, **lf**, or **sk**?

    <u>pump</u>   <u>myself</u>

    <u>grain</u>   <u>skin</u>

Write spelling words for these phonetic spellings.

24. kop′ē <u>copy</u>

25. win′dōz <u>windows</u>

26. bēnz <u>beans</u>

27. mär′kit <u>market</u>

28. sēl <u>seal</u>

29. kich′ən <u>kitchen</u>

30. ber′ēz <u>berries</u>

25

13. *ladder*   Jacob saw a *ladder* reaching to heaven.
14. *grain*   Father shoveled wheat into the *grain* bin.
15. *classes*   Spelling *classes* include taking tests.
16. *kitty*   Whose *kitty* is this?
17. *bottom*   Look in the *bottom* of your drawer.
18. *cherry*   Birds sit in our *cherry* tree.
19. *arrow*   On that map, an *arrow* points north.
20. *stream*   After the rain, the *stream* was high.
21. *peaches*   How beautiful the *peaches* look.
22. *turkey*   Mother roasted the *turkey* for dinner.
23. *whose*   A man *whose* name was Job lost all his possessions.
24. *berries*   "Can the fig tree . . . bear olive *berries?*"
25. *buggy*   Ann pushed her doll *buggy* on the porch.

B. Using Your Words Review

Fill in the puzzle with words that have the meanings given. Print one letter in each block, using capital letters. All the words are NEW WORDS in Lessons 1–5.

1. Pile of many things.
2. God's Word.
3. Person who knows and likes another.
4. Openings in walls to let in light.
5. Twigs and boughs.
6. The town where Jesus was born.
7. Fathers, mothers, and their children.
8. Room where food is cooked.
9. Have or feel pain.
10. Underground parts of plants.
11. The direction of the sunset.
12. From each pair of words, write the word that comes first in alphabetical order. Remember that when the first letter in two words is the same, you must look at the second letter in both words.

arrow	another	another
ready	rabbit	rabbit
north	number	north
field	flame	field

13. Write the following words in alphabetical order. You will need to look at the second or third letters.

Puzzle:
1. HEAP
2. BIBLE
3. FRIEND
4. WINDOWS
5. BRANCHES
6. BETHLEHEM
7. FAMILIES
8. KITCHEN
9. SUFFER
10. ROOTS
11. WEST

chimney	cash
copy	cherry
cash	chimney
classes	chop
churches	churches
cities	cities
cherry	classes
chop	cloud
coast	coast
cloud	copy

26

26. *roots* — "They saw the fig tree dried up from the *roots*."
27. *chop* — Mother wants us to *chop* the nuts finer.
28. *hundred* — A century is a *hundred* years.
29. *steam* — See the *steam* rising from the pond.
30. *weeds* — Jonah had *weeds* wrapped around his head.
31. *rabbit* — A *rabbit* was called a hare in Bible times.
32. *together* — Two men walked *together* to Emmaus.
33. *shape* — Aaron made an idol the *shape* of a calf.
34. *hammer* — No *hammer* was heard at the temple.
35. *unless* — We will come *unless* we call.
36. *soup* — Who wants tomato *soup* for supper?
37. *seal* — Do not forget to *seal* the envelope.
38. *breath* — God breathed into man the *breath* of life.

C. Building Words Review

1. To spell most plural nouns, add __s__ to the singular noun. Write the plurals of **dollar**, **load**, **field**, and **arrow**.

_____dollars_____   _____fields_____

_____loads_____   _____arrows_____

2. To spell a plural noun that ends with /iz/, add __es__ to the singular noun. Write the plurals of **class**, **peach**, **ash**, and **fuzz**.

_____classes_____   _____ashes_____

_____peaches_____   _____fuzzes_____

3. To write the plural of a noun that ends with **y** preceded by a consonant, change __y__ to __i__ and add **-es**. Write the plurals of **city**, **berry**, **story**, and **family**.

_____cities_____   _____stories_____

_____berries_____   _____families_____

4. To write the plural of a noun that ends with **y** preceded by a vowel, keep the **y** and just add __s__. Write the plurals of **tray**, **turkey**, **birthday**, and **chimney**.

_____trays_____   _____birthdays_____

_____turkeys_____   _____chimneys_____

5. Write these words, and write the number of syllables in each word.

hundred _____hundred_____ __2__

heap _____heap_____ __1__

Bethlehem _____Bethlehem_____ __3__

6. Write these words. Put slashes between the syllables according to the VC/CV pattern

suffer _____suf/fer_____

market _____mar/ket_____

windows _____win/dows_____

7. Write these words and put slashes between the syllables. The pattern is VC/V because the first vowel is (<u>short</u>, long).

study _____stud/y_____

copy _____cop/y_____

robin _____rob/in_____

8. Write these words and put slashes between the syllables. The pattern is V/CV because the first vowel is (short, <u>long</u>).

tulip _____tu/lip_____

station _____sta/tion_____

wafers _____wa/fers_____

9. In each of these words, the suffix is a new syllable. Write the words. Put slashes between the root words and suffixes.

patches _____patch/es_____

benches _____bench/es_____

Bible Thoughts

Use a spelling word to complete this sentence.

10. Jesus told the disciples, "I am the vine, ye are the _____branches_____" (John 15:5).

C. 41 points

39.	*branches*	All the *branches* are hanging low.
40.	*stories*	Both *stories* were about blind people.
41.	*match*	This sock does not *match* that one.
42.	*patch*	Between the clouds is a *patch* of blue sky.
43.	*staff*	A music *staff* has five lines.
44.	*pitch*	Blow the *pitch* on the pitch pipe.
45.	*station*	The train left the *station* on time.
46.	*cities*	Those two *cities* are far apart.
47.	*heathen*	Many *heathen* people have no Bibles.
48.	*Bethlehem*	David lived in *Bethlehem* long ago.
49.	*tulip*	Next spring the *tulip* bulbs will grow.
50.	*Bible*	The *Bible* has sixty-six books.

LESSON 7

b/e/ll

r/a/bbits

NEW WORDS

opened   remember
melted   instead
dressed   breakfast
ordered   Ezra
acted   Esther Esth.
death   Exodus Ex.
health   Daniel Dan.
heaven   Genesis Gen.

REVIEW WORDS

packed   feathers
planted   again

A. Sounds and Letters

- The vowel sound /a/, as in **apple**, is usually spelled with the letter **a**.
  p<u>a</u>ck   **pl<u>a</u>nt**

1. In which Bible book name from the spelling word list do you hear /a/ in the first syllable? _____Daniel_____

2. Which other spelling words have /a/ in the first syllable? Be careful. Do not write every word that has the letter **a**.

_____acted_____ _____planted_____
_____packed_____

- The vowel sound /e/, as in **egg**, is usually spelled with the letter **e**.
  m<u>e</u>lt   **dr<u>e</u>ss**
  In some words, /e/ is spelled with the digraph **ea**.
  h<u>ea</u>ven   **d<u>ea</u>th**

3. Which Bible book names from the spelling list begin with /e/? _____Ezra_____
_____Esther_____ _____Exodus_____
Which other Bible book name has /e/ within the first syllable? _____Genesis_____

4. Which other NEW WORDS have /e/ spelled **e**? (Do not write **opened**.) _____melted_____
_____dressed_____ _____remember_____

5. Which spelling words have /e/ spelled with the digraph **ea**?

_____death_____ _____instead_____
_____health_____ _____breakfast_____
_____heaven_____ _____feathers_____

6. Which REVIEW WORD has the consonant blend **nt**? _____planted_____

A. 27 points

28

Test Sentences

1.	*heaven*	The stars are between *heaven* and earth.
2.	*melted*	When the sun got hot, the manna *melted*.
3.	*acted*	The opossum *acted* as though it were dead.
4.	*dressed*	Abraham *dressed* a calf for his visitors.
5.	*instead*	They use margarine *instead* of butter.
6.	*death*	We need not face *death* fearfully.
7.	*breakfast*	A good *breakfast* gives you energy.
8.	*health*	Good *health* is a blessing.
9.	*ordered*	Last week Father *ordered* a new suit.
10.	*remember*	Jesus told us to *remember* Lot's wife.
11.	*opened*	Samuel *opened* the doors of the temple.
12.	*Ezra*	We read in *Ezra* of rebuilding the temple.

Write spelling words for these phonetic spellings.

7. ə gen′ _____ again _____

8. ri mem′bər _____ remember _____

9. in sted′ _____ instead _____

10. deth _____ death _____

11. brek′fəst _____ breakfast _____

12. hev′ən _____ heaven _____

13. Write the root word of **dressed**. Then write its plural form.

_____ dress _____   _____ dresses _____

14. In which NEW WORD do you see the word **pen**? _____ opened _____

B. Using Your Words

B. 23 points

Fill in the blanks with spelling words from the first column.

The shortest verse in the Bible says, "Jesus wept" (John 11:35). Jesus was sad when He heard about the **(1)** _____ death _____ of Lazarus. Already Lazarus was buried. His grave was a cave. The cave could be **(2)** _____ opened _____ by removing a stone at the entrance. Jesus went to the cave, looked up toward **(3)** _____ heaven _____, and prayed. Then He **(4)** _____ ordered _____ Lazarus to come forth. Lazarus came out **(5)** _____ dressed _____ in grave clothes. A napkin was on his face, and the rest of his body was wrapped in bands of linen cloth. Jesus said, "Loose him, and let him go."

6. Write two sentences of your own. Use **opened** and **breakfast** in the first sentence. Use **packed** and **feathers** in the second sentence.

a. _____ (Individual sentences) _____

b. _____

7. Fill in the blanks with spelling words.

a. Roland _____ packed _____ all the books into boxes.

b. Jesus restored Peter's wife's mother to good _____ health _____ .

c. Jesus will come to earth _____ again _____ .

d. Abraham offered a ram _____ instead _____ of Isaac.

e. The hot sun _____ melted _____ the manna that God had sent.

29

For numbers 13–16, write the Bible book name *and* its abbreviation.

13. *Esther*   *Esth.*   The Book of *Esther* precedes Job.
14. *Exodus*   *Ex.*   In *Exodus* we read about Moses.
15. *Daniel*   *Dan.*   The Book of *Daniel* follows Ezekiel.
16. *Genesis*   *Gen.*   Read in *Genesis* about the Creation.

Both sentences this time are questions. So end them with question marks.

Who *packed feathers* into this box?

Have you *planted* beans *again?*

f. Nebuchadnezzar's hair grew like eagles'

<u>   feathers   </u> .

g. Some farmers <u>   planted   </u> their

corn seed by hand.

h. We have family devotions after eating

<u>   breakfast   </u> .

8. Five NEW WORDS are names of Bible books.
Write them in alphabetical order.

<u>   Daniel   </u>

<u>   Esther   </u>

<u>   Exodus   </u>

<u>   Ezra   </u>

<u>   Genesis   </u>

~~~~~~~~~ **An Interesting Word** ~~~~~~~~~

9. A **fast** is a time when a person does not eat.
One meaning of **break** is "to end" or "to
stop." **Breakfast** is the meal a person eats
when he ends the fast he had during the
night. Write **breakfast**.

<u>   breakfast   </u>

~~~~~~

C. Building Words

[smell][ed]

- **Verb Forms**
  Many verbs that show past
  action end with a /d/, /t/, or
  /id/ suffix. To spell these verbs,
  add **-ed** to the present forms.
  smell + /d/ = smelled
  pack + /t/ = packed
  melt + /id/ = melted

1. A word that shows action is a **verb**. Some
verbs show action that is happening now.

The dogs **roll** on the grass.

We **pick** the red tomatoes.

From the list OF NEW WORDS, find the verb
that completes this sentence.

Now I <u> remember </u> your name.

2. Some verbs show action that happened in
the past. Many of these verbs are built from
verbs that show present action.

[pack][ed]   **[melt][ed]**

roll + /d/   The dogs **rolled** on the grass.

pick + /t/   We **picked** the red tomatoes.

paint + /id/   Father **painted** the house.

What sounds are added to verbs to show

past action? <u>/d/</u> <u>/t/</u> <u>/id/</u> What two

letters spell these sounds? <u>   ed   </u>

3. The **-ed** ending is a suffix that shows past
action. Complete these sentences by writing the boldface verbs and adding the suffix **-ed** to spell the sounds shown.

a. **order** + /d/   Jesus <u> ordered </u>

the servants to fill the waterpots.

b. **open** + /d/   God <u> opened </u> the

windows of heaven and sent the Flood.

c. **plant** + /id/   Jesus told a parable about a

man who <u> planted </u> a vineyard.

C. 31 points

d. **act** + /id/   Uncle Luke ___acted___ as though he were tired.

e. **melt** + /id/   The snow on the mountains had ___melted___ by July 1.

f. **dress** + /t/   We ___dressed___ in our warm stockings and mittens.

g. **pack** + /t/   Who has ___packed___ this box?

• **Abbreviations**
Most abbreviations end with periods.   **Gen.   Ex.**
An abbreviation begins with a capital letter if the word for which it stands begins with a capital letter.   **Daniel—Dan.**

---

4. To save time and space, we sometimes write a short form of a word. Several letters that stand for a whole word are an **abbreviation**. Look at the spelling list. What is the short way of writing **Exodus**?

___Ex.___

5. Many of the long Bible book names may be abbreviated, but the short names should not be abbreviated. Which Bible book name in the spelling list has no abbreviation beside it?

___Ezra___

6. Write the other Bible book names from the spelling list. Beside each name, write its abbreviation.

Esther	Esth.
Exodus	Ex.
Daniel	Dan.
Genesis	Gen.

7. The names for books of the Bible always begin with capital letters because they name specific (places, <u>things</u>). An abbreviation for a Bible book name also begins with a (small, <u>capital</u>) letter.

8. Write the abbreviations from the list again.

Esth.	Dan.
Ex.	Gen.

Bible Thoughts

Write the answers.

9. In the Hebrew language, the syllable **el** means **God**. Many names end with **el**, such as **Ezekiel** and **Bethel**. Write the Bible book name from the spelling words that ends with **el**.

___Daniel___

10. Matthew 1:23 gives a name for Jesus that ends with **el** and means "God with us." Write this name.

___Emmanuel___

11. Which of the spelling words names the first book of the Bible?

___Genesis___

42 Grade 4 Spelling

LESSON 8

NEW WORDS

dropped   slipped
shipped   printed
watched   lock
wanted   blanket
begged   minister
visited   minute
planned   doctor
finished   Dr.

REVIEW WORDS

bother   Mr.
Miss   Mrs.

A. Sounds and Letters

> • The vowel sound /i/, as in **igloo**, is usually spelled **i**.
> **pr**i**nt**   **v**i**s**i**t**
> Sometimes /i/ is spelled **e**.
> **pock**e**t**

1. Which spelling words have /i/ spelled **i**? (Do not write **Mr.** or **Mrs.**)

   shipped   printed
   visited   minister
   finished   minute
   slipped   Miss

p/i/ckles

s/o/cks

2. Of the words you wrote for number 1, which have two **i**'s? _____ finished _____
   _____ visited _____ minister _____

3. In the two-syllable word **minute**, the vowel sound in both syllables is /i/. What letter spells /i/ in the first syllable? __i__ In the second syllable? __u__

4. What letter spells /i/ in the second syllable of **blanket**? __e__

> • The vowel sound /o/, as in **top**, is usually spelled **o**. **dr**o**p** **l**o**ck**
> Often when /o/ comes after **w**, /o/ is spelled **a**. **w**a**nt** **w**a**sh**

5. Which spelling words have /o/ spelled **o**?
   dropped   doctor
   lock   bother

6. Which spelling words have /o/ spelled **a**?
   watched   wanted
   What letter comes before **a** in these words?
   __w__

7. Write **planned**. _____ planned _____
   It has the vowel sound (/a/, /e/, /i/, /o/, /u/).

A. 32 points

32

Test Sentences

1.	*blanket*	A *blanket* of snow covered the ground.
2.	*slipped*	The little boy *slipped* and fell.
3.	*printed*	This book was *printed* in Kentucky.
4.	*planned*	Mother had *planned* to bake today.
5.	*dropped*	Sharon had *dropped* her scarf.
6.	*minute*	Do you have a *minute* to spare?
7.	*lock*	Please *lock* the door when you leave.
8.	*visited*	Paul *visited* the churches he helped to establish.
9.	*minister*	Listen when the *minister* is preaching.
10.	*shipped*	The package was *shipped* to the school.
11.	*finished*	Who *finished* doing the dishes?
12.	*watched*	We have *watched* long enough.

8. Write **again**. ___again___ What letters spell /e/? __ai__

9. Write the NEW WORDS that ended with /ch/ or /sh/ before the suffix **-ed** was added.

___watched___   ___finished___

One of these words has the /ch/ sound. What three letters spell that sound? __tch__

Write spelling words for these phonetic spellings.

10. dok′tər ___doctor___

11. bo_th_′ər ___bother___

12. begd ___begged___

13. shipt ___shipped___

B. Using Your Words

When Naomi returned to Bethlehem with Ruth, the farmers were harvesting barley. Ruth went to glean in the field after the reapers (Ruth 2:3). Gleaning is gathering what the reapers leave behind when they have **(1)** ___finished___ cutting grain. The reapers were not to **(2)** ___bother___ cutting all the grain in the corners of the field. Sometimes they even **(3)** ___dropped___ some grain on purpose. God **(4)** ___wanted___ the strangers, widows, and poor people to have food to eat. So He **(5)** ___planned___ that they could glean in the fields.

6. Write two sentences of your own. Use **watched** and **minister** in the first sentence. Use **lock** and **bother** in the second sentence.

a. _____(Individual sentences.)_____
b. _____

Fill in the blanks with spelling words.

7. **School** is to **teacher** as **church** is to ___minister___.

8. **Post office** is to **postman** as **hospital** is to ___doctor___.

9. **Week** is to **day** as **hour** is to ___minute___.

10. **House** is to **roof** as **bed** is to ___blanket___.

11. **Nose** is to **smelled** as **eye** is to ___watched___.

33

B. 26 points

Explain the thinking process for these analogies. For example, an overseer in a *school* is a *teacher*. An overseer in a *church* is a ———.

13. *wanted*   Zacchaeus *wanted* to see Jesus.
14. *begged*   The lame man sat and *begged* for alms.
15. *doctor*   God gives the *doctor* wisdom.

Write the abbreviation for *doctor*.
16. *Dr.*   *(doctor)*   Do you know *Dr.* Nagle?

Both sentences this time are questions. So end them with question marks.

Did *Miss* Esther *bother* you?

Will *Mr.* and *Mrs.* Daniel bring candy?

12. Cake is to **baked** as **book** is to

_____printed_____ .

13. Envelope is to **seal** as **door** is to

_____lock_____ .

14. Write the spelling words that are titles for these people. All but one are abbreviations.

a. a man _____Mr._____

b. a married woman _____Mrs._____

c. an unmarried woman _____Miss_____

d. someone who helps the sick _____Dr._____

15. Write these words in alphabetical order.

miss	lock
lock	minister
minister	minute
printed	miss
planned	planned
minute	printed

C. Building Words

• **Verb Forms**

When adding **-ed** to a verb to make it show past tense, double the final consonant of a root word that has one syllable, has one vowel, and ends with one consonant. **beg + /d/ = begged**
drop + /t/ = dropped

1. Fill in the blanks in the sentences below with past tense forms of these words.

beg drop slip plan stop ship

a. The dish ____slipped____ from my hand.

b. The bishops ____planned____ the meeting.

c. The temperature ____dropped____ ten degrees.

d. Bananas are ____shipped____ green.

e. Bartimaeus ____begged____ for money.

f. Jesus ____stopped____ and called for Bartimaeus.

2. The words **visit** and **cover** have two syllables. Add **-ed** without doubling the final consonant.

____visited____   ____covered____

3. Print, **watch**, and **lock** end with more than one consonant. Add **-ed** without doubling the final consonant. ____printed____

____watched____   ____locked____

4. Complete these sentences with verbs showing past action. Use the suffix **-ed** to add the /d/, /t/, and /id/ sounds to the boldface verbs.

a. **bother** + /d/   My sore thumb bothered me when I wrote.

b. **finish** + /t/   On the cross Jesus said, "It is __finished__."

c. **want** + /id/   Daniel ____wanted____ water rather than wine.

C. 25 points

34

5. Write the spelling words that are abbreviations for these titles.

Mistress <u>Mrs.</u>   Mister <u>Mr.</u>

Doctor <u>Dr.</u>

6. Each abbreviation in number 5 above begins with a <u>capital</u> letter and ends with a <u>period</u>.

• **Abbreviations**
The abbreviation **Dr.** should be used only with a name.
   Ask **Dr.** George Wells.
   Ask the **doctor**.
---

7. Write **doctor** or **Dr.** in each blank.

a. We are going to see <u>Dr.</u> John Long.

b. He is always a kind and careful <u>doctor</u>.

8. Which spelling word is the title for a girl or a woman who is not married?

<u>Miss</u>

9. The word you wrote for number 8 is not an abbreviation, so it ends (with, <u>without</u>) a period.

Bible Thoughts

Write the answers.

10. **Doctor** comes from the Latin word **doceo**, which means "teach." When **doctor** was first used in the English language, it meant "a person who teaches." Luke 2:46 says that Jesus was in the temple with the doctors. That means Jesus was with the teachers. Write **doctor**.

<u>doctor</u>

11. Read Exodus 24:13. In this verse, find one of the spelling words that means **servant** as it is used in that verse.

<u>minister</u>

LESSON 9

NEW WORDS

says	*punish*
becomes	*covet*
country	*Judges Judg.*
blood	*Numbers Num.*
wondered	*Proverbs Prov.*
trouble	*Joshua Josh.*
touch	*2 Samuel 2 Sam.*
rushed	*1 Timothy 1 Tim.*

br/u/shes
d/u/cklings

REVIEW WORDS

button	*thinks*
covers	*teaches*

A. Sounds and Letters

> • The most common spelling of /u/, as in **cup**, is **u**.
>
>   **b**u**tton   r**u**sh**
>
>   Other spellings of /u/ are **o**, **ou**, and **oo**.
>
>   **c**o**ver   t**ou**ch   bl**oo**d**

1. Write the correct spelling words for these clues. On the short blanks, write the letters that spell /u/ in the words you write.

   a. rhymes with **double**

      ____trouble____   __ou__

   b. rhymes with **gushed**

      ____rushed____   __u__

   c. rhymes with **hums**

      ____becomes____   __o__

   d. rhymes with **much**

      ____touch____   __ou__

   e. ends like **fish**

      ____punish____   __u__

   f. begins like **wagon**

      ____wondered____   __o__

   g. last syllable sounds like **tree**

      ____country____   __ou__

2. Write the REVIEW WORD that has a double consonant in the middle. Then write the letter that spells /u/ in the first syllable.

   ____button____   __u__

3. Write the NEW WORD that rhymes with **flood**, and the two letters that spell /u/.

   ____blood____   __oo__

4. Find the NEW WORD and the REVIEW WORD that begin with the same four letters.

   ____covet____   ____covers____

   In both words, /u/ is spelled __o__.

A. 36 points

36

Test Sentences

1.	*touch*	Feathers feel smooth when you *touch* them.
2.	*blood*	Christ shed His *blood* on the cross.
3.	*becomes*	A chrysalis *becomes* a butterfly.
4.	*rushed*	The child was *rushed* to the hospital.
5.	*trouble*	"God is . . . a very present help in *trouble*."
6.	*covet*	We should not *covet* other people's things.
7.	*punish*	Parents must *punish* disobedient children.
8.	*country*	People move to this *country* every day.
9.	*wondered*	Rhoda *wondered* who was knocking.
10.	*says*	Jesus *says*, "Come unto me."

5. Which NEW WORDS name books of the Bible with the /u/ sound?

_____Judges_____   _____Numbers_____

In both words, /u/ is spelled __u__.

6. Which spelling words have /sh/?

_____rushed_____   _____punish_____

_____Joshua_____

7. Which spelling words have /ch/?

_____touch_____   _____teaches_____

Write spelling words for these phonetic spellings.

8. sez _____says_____

9. kuv′ərz _____covers_____

10. kuv′it _____covet_____

11. josh′ o͞o ə _____Joshua_____

12. juj′iz _____Judges_____

13. but′ən _____button_____

14. rusht _____rushed_____

B. 31 points

B. Using Your Words

Fill in the blanks with spelling words from the first column.

When Jesus healed a certain sick man, He said, "Arise, and take up thy bed, and go thy way into thine house" (Mark 2:11). The next verse **(1)** _____says_____ that the man did that. Have you **(2)** _____wondered_____ how one man could carry his bed? In those days people slept on mats spread on the floor. The coats that the people wore during the day served as **(3)** _____covers_____ at night. When not in use, the mats could be rolled up. Now it **(4)** _____becomes_____ easier to understand why it was no **(5)** _____trouble_____ for this man to carry his bed.

6. Write two sentences of your own. Use **covet** and **punish** in the first sentence. Use **trouble** and **touch** in the second sentence.

a. _____(Individual sentences.)_____

b. _____

Fill in the blanks with spelling words.

7. **Atlantic** is to **ocean** as **Canada** is to

_____country_____.

8. **Ear** is to **hear** as **finger** is to

_____touch_____.

9. **Hose** is to **water** as **vein** is to

_____blood_____.

37

For numbers 11–16, write the Bible book name *and* its abbreviation.

11.	*Judges*	*Judg.*	We read in *Judges* about Samson.
12.	*Numbers*	*Num.*	Moses wrote the Book of *Numbers*.
13.	*Proverbs*	*Prov.*	The Book of *Proverbs* has wise counsel.
14.	*Joshua*	*Josh.*	Chapter 2 of *Joshua* tells about Rahab.
15.	*2 Samuel*	*2 Sam.*	We read in *2 Samuel* about David.
16.	*1 Timothy*	*1 Tim.*	Paul wrote *1 Timothy* to Timothy.

One sentence ends with a period, and one ends with a question mark. You must decide which ends with which.

Who *thinks* the *covers* are warm?

Mother *teaches* him to *button* his shirt.

10. The words **wondered** and **wandered** are sometimes confused. Which word means "wished to know"? _____wondered_____ Which word means "went about without any special purpose"? ___wandered___

11. Write **wondered** or **wandered**.

a. I __wondered__ what I could do to help.

b. How long had the Israelites _wandered_ in the wilderness?

c. The little lamb __wandered__ away from the flock.

d. After our work was finished, we __wandered__ in the woods.

e. The boys __wondered__ where Gaza is.

12. Write these words in alphabetical order.

country	blood
city	cherry
blood	city
covet	country
cherry	cover
cover	covet

13. Which book follows each of these in the Bible?

1 Samuel	2 Samuel
Leviticus	Numbers
Psalms	Proverbs
Joshua	Judges
2 Thessalonians	1 Timothy
Deuteronomy	Joshua

C. Building Words

• **Verb Forms**
When /z/ or /s/ is added to a verb, the suffix is spelled **-s**.
become + /z/ = becomes
think + /s/ = thinks

1. Add a /z/ or /s/ suffix to each underlined word. Spell this suffix with the letter **s**.

a. I think you may. Mother ___thinks___ you may.

b. Christian women cover their heads. A Christian woman ___covers___ her head.

c. Sometimes people covet. Anyone who ___covets___ should remember the tenth commandment.

d. You button your coat. He ___buttons___ his coat.

• When /iz/ is added to a verb, the suffix is spelled **-es**. This adds another syllable to the word.
teach + /iz/ = teaches

C. 24 points

38

rush + /iz/ = rushes

2. Add the /iz/ suffix to each underlined word. Spell this suffix with the letters **es**.

a. Our parents <u>teach</u>. Our teacher
   <u>teaches</u> .

b. The branches <u>touch</u> each other. One branch <u>touches</u> the house.

c. Sometimes parents <u>punish</u> children. A father <u>punishes</u> his disobedient son.

d. Hear the water <u>rush</u>. It <u>rushes</u> noisily.

3. In Bible book names, we write **1** for **First** and **2** for **Second**.   **1 Kings   2 Kings**

Write the following names correctly.

First Timothy _____<u>1 Timothy</u>_____

Second Samuel _____<u>2 Samuel</u>_____

4. Write the spelling words that are Bible book names. Beside them, write their abbreviations.

Judges	Judg.
Numbers	Num.
Proverbs	Prov.
Joshua	Josh.
2 Samuel	2 Sam.
1 Timothy	1 Tim.

Bible Thoughts

Write the answers.

5. Which spelling word names a book of the Bible and ends with **el**?

   _____2 Samuel_____

6. Who wrote many of the wise sayings in the Book of Proverbs? Read Proverbs 1:1 and 10:1 if you need help.

   _____Solomon_____

39

LESSON 10

NEW WORDS

cheese   shopping
peace   Sunday Sun.
preach   Monday Mon.
raise   Tuesday Tues.
grapes   Wednesday Wed.
create   Thursday Thur.
reaches   Friday Fri.
painting   Saturday Sat.

REVIEW WORDS

clay   steal
heavy   steel

s/ā/lboat   l/ē/ves

A. Sounds and Letters

> • Common spellings of the vowel sound /ā/, as in **cake**, are **a**, **a-e**, **ai**, and **ay**.
>   p**a**per   gr**a**p**e**   p**ai**nt   cl**ay**
> At the end of a word, /ā/ is usually spelled **ay**. s**ay** del**ay**

1. In **game**, /ā/ is spelled with the split digraph **a-e**. This means **a**, then any consonant, and then **e**. Which plural spelling word has /ā/ spelled with the split digraph **a-e**?

          grapes

2. In which NEW WORDS is /ā/ spelled **ai**?

   raise   painting

3. Write the spelling word in which the first syllable ends with /ē/ and the second syllable begins with /ā/.   create

4. Which REVIEW WORD ends with /ā/?

   clay   What letters spell /ā/ at the end of a word?   ay

> • Common spellings of the vowel sound /ē/, as in **tree**, are **e**, **ee**, and **ea**. **e**ven ch**ee**se r**ea**ch When /ē/ ends the last syllable of a word, /ē/ is often spelled **y**. bod**y** heav**y**

5. In which spelling words does /ē/ have these spellings?

e   create

ee   cheese   steel

ea   peace   reaches
     preach   steal

6. Write the names of the days of the week.

   Sunday   Thursday

   Monday   Friday

   Tuesday   Saturday

   Wednesday

A. 29 points

40

Test Sentences

1. *grapes*   Our purple *grapes* ripen in September.
2. *preach*   The ministers *preach* God's Word.
3. *reaches*   Our land *reaches* to that row of trees.
4. *raise*   Our cousins *raise* popcorn every year.
5. *shopping*   Mother went *shopping* on Saturday.
6. *cheese*   Eat *cheese* for a good source of protein.
7. *peace*   Great *peace* have they who love God's Law.
8. *painting*   Father is *painting* the barn.
9. *create*   On which day did God *create* the birds?

7. In the names of the days of the week, the last syllable is pronounced /dā/. What two letters spell the vowel sound in this syllable? __ay__

8. Which REVIEW WORD ends with /ē/? ____heavy____ What letter spells /ē/? __y__

9. Which NEW WORD has the digraph **sh**?

_____shopping_____

Write spelling words for these phonetic spellings.

10. wenz′dā′ _____Wednesday_____

11. tōōz′dā′ _____Tuesday_____

12. chēz _____cheese_____

13. stēl (two words) _____steal_____

_____steel_____

B. Using Your Words

B. 21 points

Fill in the blanks with spelling words from the first column.

Pottery making was important work in Bible times. To make a vessel, a potter first steps on some clay until it is just right for molding. Next, he will **(1)** ____raise____ the pile of **(2)** ____clay____ onto a wooden wheel. This wheel has an axle that **(3)** ____reaches____ down to a lower wooden wheel. The potter makes the top wheel spin by turning the **(4)** ____heavy____ bottom wheel with his foot. He uses his hands to shape the vessel. Sometimes the potter will make the vessel more attractive by **(5)** ____painting____ a design on it.

6. Write two sentences of your own. Use **preach** and **Sunday** in the first sentence. Use **cheese** and **steal** in the second sentence.

a. _____(Individual sentences.)_____

b. _____

7. Write the spelling words that mean the same as the underlined words.

a. Jay ate <u>solid food made from milk</u> with his crackers. _____cheese_____

b. We like juice made from <u>fruit that grows on a vine.</u> _____grapes_____

c. God simply spoke words to <u>make</u> the world <u>from nothing.</u> _____create_____

41

For numbers 10–16, write the name of the day of the week *and* its abbreviation.

10. *Sunday*   *Sun.*   A visitor preached *Sunday* evening.
11. *Monday*   *Mon.*   Mother washes clothes on *Monday* morning.
12. *Tuesday*   *Tues.*   Every *Tuesday* she does the ironing.
13. *Wednesday*   *Wed.*   Last *Wednesday* we were at school.
14. *Thursday*   *Thur.*   Thanksgiving is on *Thursday* each year.
15. *Friday*   *Fri.*   Good *Friday* is before Easter.
16. *Saturday*   *Sat.*   On *Saturday* we help to work at home.

One sentence ends with a period, and one ends with a question mark. You must decide which ends with which.

Why did he *steal* the *clay* ball?

She dropped the *heavy steel* pipe.

d. Yesterday we went <u>visiting stores to buy</u>

<u>things</u> with Mother. ____shopping____

8. Two REVIEW WORDS are homophones. Write the correct one in each blank.

a. Iron is mixed with carbon to make

____steel____.

b. The Bible says, "Thou shalt not

____steal____" (Exodus 20:15).

c. A ____steel____ bridge crosses the river.

9. Which NEW WORD is a homophone for **piece**?

____peace____ Write the correct homophone in each blank.

a. Use a clean ____piece____ of paper for the test.

b. Christians try to live in ____peace____ with other people.

c. War is the opposite of ____peace____.

d. Peter took a ____piece____ of money from the fish's mouth.

C. Building Words

C. 46 points

> **• Suffixes**
> When adding a suffix that begins with a vowel, double the final consonant of a root word that
>   has one syllable,
>   has one vowel, and
>   ends with a single consonant.
>   **cut + /ing/ = cutting**

1. Add **-ing** to the following words, using the rule above.

shop ____shopping____

put ____putting____

get ____getting____

nod ____nodding____

skip ____skipping____

plan ____planning____

swim ____swimming____

2. Add **-ing** to the following words. You will not double the final consonant.

paint ____painting____

preach ____preaching____

steal ____stealing____

wonder ____wondering____

3. Write each word, adding the suffix **-s** or **-es** to it.

count ____counts____

reach ____reaches____

wash ____washes____

steal ____steals____

match ____matches____

4. Write the names of the days of the week. After each name, write its abbreviation twice.

Sunday	Sun.	Sun.
Monday	Mon.	Mon.
Tuesday	Tues.	Tues.
Wednesday	Wed.	Wed.
Thursday	Thur.	Thur.
Friday	Fri.	Fri.
Saturday	Sat.	Sat.

Dictionary Practice

5. The entry words in a dictionary show how to divide words into syllables. Here is an example: **dif fer ent**.

Find the following words in the Speller Dictionary, and write each one in syllables as shown in the entry word. Use slashes to show the syllable divisions.

heavy	heav/y
covet	cov/et
create	cre/ate
Sunday	Sun/day
cheese	cheese
minister	min/is/ter
Wednesday	Wednes/day

Bible Thoughts

Use spelling words to complete these sentences.

6. Ephesians 4:28 says, "Let him that stole _____ steal _____ no more."

7. We go to church on the first day of the week (Acts 20:7). We call this day _____ Sunday _____.

LESSON 11

NEW WORDS

throwing

sewing

changing

tried

bowl

closed

created

invite

hello

strike

shining

tries

float

oatmeal

studied

climbed

sk/ī/

sn/ō/

REVIEW WORDS

might

bright

coast

pages

A. Sounds and Letters

> • Common spellings of the vowel sound /ī/, as in **kite**, are **i**, **i-e**, **igh**, and **y**.
> cl<u>i</u>mb inv<u>i</u>t<u>e</u> m<u>igh</u>t tr<u>y</u>

1. Which spelling words are forms of **try**?

   _____tried_____   _____tries_____

   How was /ī/ spelled before the suffixes were added? _y_

2. Which spelling word is a form of **shine**?

   _____shining_____ What split digraph spelled /ī/ before the suffix was added? _i-e_

In which other spelling words is /ī/ spelled like /ī/ in **shine**?

   _____invite_____   _____strike_____

3. In which spelling words is /ī/ spelled **igh**?

   _____might_____   _____bright_____

4. Write the spelling word that is pronounced /klīmd/. _climbed_ What letter spells /ī/? _i_ What consonant follows **m**? _b_

> • Common spellings of the vowel sound /ō/, as in **boat**, are **o**, **o-e**, **oa**, and **ow**.
> hell<u>o</u> cl<u>o</u>s<u>e</u> <u>oa</u>ts b<u>ow</u>l

5. In which spelling words does /ō/ have these spellings?

   o _____hello_____   **o-e** _____closed_____

   ow _____throwing_____   _____bowl_____

   oa _____float_____   _____oatmeal_____

   _____coast_____

6. Write the spelling word that rhymes with **throwing**. _sewing_ What diagraph spells /ō/ in this word? _ew_

A. 27 points

44

Test Sentences

1.	*invite*	Mother will *invite* guests for dinner.
2.	*strike*	If someone harms you, do not *strike* him.
3.	*shining*	The sun was *shining* brightly.
4.	*float*	A light object will *float* on water.
5.	*bowl*	We gave a *bowl* of fruit to Grandmother.
6.	*oatmeal*	Did you eat *oatmeal* for breakfast?
7.	*studied*	Martin diligently *studied* God's Word.
8.	*tries*	Baby sister *tries* to walk.
9.	*throwing*	The children were *throwing* the ball.
10.	*sewing*	My sister is *sewing* a dress.
11.	*closed*	Noah went in, and God *closed* the door.
12.	*created*	God *created* man on the sixth day.

7. Which spelling word has a double consonant? _____hello_____

**Write spelling words for these phonetic
spellings.**

8. krē āt'id _____created_____

9. bōl _____bowl_____

10. pāj'iz _____pages_____

11. kōst _____coast_____

12. ōt'mēl' _____oatmeal_____

B. 21 points

B. Using Your Words

Fill in the blanks with spelling words from the first column.

In Bible times, **(1)** ___changing___ wheat to flour for baking bread was not an easy

task. After the wheat was threshed, it had to be winnowed. Winnowing was done by

(2) ___throwing___ the straw, chaff, and wheat into the air. A breeze carried away the

chaff and straw, and the wheat fell to the ground. Before Mother could use the wheat,

she sifted out the pebbles and seeds of tares. Then Mother was ready to start grinding.

She put the wheat into a stone **(3)** ___bowl___ called a mortar and ground it with

a pestle. She **(4)** ___tried___ to grind it very fine. She **(5)** ___might___ have

worked for several hours before she had enough flour to bake bread.

6. Write two sentences of your own. Use **pages** and **studied** in the first sentence. Use **tried** and **changing** in the second sentence.

a. _____(Individual sentences.)_____

b. _____

7. Words that have opposite meanings are
called **antonyms**. Write the spelling words
that are antonyms of the boldface words.

a. **good-bye** Instead of saying ___hello___,
Boaz said, "The LORD be with you."

b. **sink** People ___float___ easily in
the Dead Sea, which is the saltiest body

of water in the world.

c. **destroyed** God ___created___ the
world in six days.

d. **catching** Shimei was ___throwing___
stones at David and cursing him.

45

13. *changing*   Fall is *changing* to winter.
14. *tried*   Everyone *tried* to catch the rabbit.
15. *climbed*   Zacchaeus *climbed* a tree to see Jesus.
16. *hello*   We say *hello* to people we meet.

One sentence ends with a period, and one ends with a question mark. You must decide which
ends with which.

We *might coast* on the hill.

Were *bright* letters put on the *pages?*

e. **opened**   The gate of the dam was

_____closed_____ to raise the water level.

f. **tearing**   The cobbler used a strong thread

when _____sewing_____ the shoes.

8. Write the spelling words that are antonyms

for **dark**.

_____shining_____   _____bright_____

9. Write the spelling word that means "oats

made into meal." _____oatmeal_____

C. Building Words

• **Verb Forms**
  To add a suffix that begins with
  a vowel to a word that ends with
  a consonant and then **e**, drop the
  final **e**.   **like + ed = liked**
  shine + ing = shining

1. Add **-ed** and **-ing** to each word.

shine	_shined_	_shining_
change	_changed_	_changing_
close	_closed_	_closing_
create	_created_	_creating_
page	_paged_	_paging_
invite	_invited_	_inviting_
raise	_raised_	_raising_

2. Complete each sentence by adding **-ed** or
-ing to the boldface verb.

a. **close**   The pupils are _____closing_____

their books.

**Write spelling words that could be used
instead of the underlined words.**

10. The waves were pounding along the

seashore. _____coast_____

11. George <u>shut</u> the door. _____closed_____

12. Grace will <u>ask</u> her cousins to come to her

house. _____invite_____

b. **shine**   The light was _____shining_____

brightly.

c. **change**   Saul's name was _____changed_____

to Paul.

d. **create**   We thank God for _____creating_____

colorful flowers.

• To add a suffix to a word that
  ends with a consonant and then
  y, change the **y** to **i**.
    fly—flies   steady—steadied
  Do not change **y** to **i** when the
  suffix begins with **i**.
    flying   steadying

3. Add **-es** and **-ing** to each word.

try	_tries_	_trying_
study	_studies_	_studying_
hurry	_hurries_	_hurrying_

C. 40 points

46

4. Add **-ed** and **-ing** to each word.

carry   carried   carrying

copy   copied   copying

bury   buried   burying

• **Syllables**

When a suffix makes a new syllable, divide the word into syllables between the root word and the suffix.

   print/ed   clos/ing

---

5. Write these words. Use slashes to divide the syllables. Follow the rule above.

climbing coasted striking changing

   climb/ing   strik/ing

   coast/ed   chang/ing

6. Write these words. Use slashes to divide the syllables. Since the final consonant was doubled to add the suffix, divide between the consonants.

shopping begging padded petted

   shop/ping   pad/ded

   beg/ging   pet/ted

Bible Thoughts

Use spelling words to complete these sentences.

7. Zacchaeus ___climbed___ into a tree to see Jesus (Luke 19:4).

8. By the power of God Elisha made an ax head ___float___ (2 Kings 6:6).

47

LESSON 12

7	8	9	10	11
opened	dropped	says	cheese	throwing
melted	shipped	becomes	peace	sewing
dressed	watched	country	preach	changing
ordered	wanted	blood	raise	tried
acted	begged	touch	grapes	bowl
death	visited	trouble	create	closed
health	planned	wondered	reaches	created
heaven	finished	rushed	painting	invite
remember	slipped	punish	shopping	hello
instead	printed	covet	Sunday Sun.	strike
breakfast	lock	Judges Judg.	Monday Mon.	shining
Ezra	blanket	Numbers Num.	Tuesday Tues.	tries
Esther Esth.	minister	Proverbs Prov.	Wednesday Wed.	float
Exodus Ex.	minute	Joshua Josh.	Thursday Thur.	oatmeal
Daniel Dan.	doctor	2 Samuel 2 Sam.	Friday Fri.	studied
Genesis Gen.	Dr.	1 Timothy 1 Tim.	Saturday Sat.	climbed

A. Sounds and Letters Review

A. 36 points

1. Write two Lesson 7 words that have the /a/ sound in the first syllable.

   <u>acted</u> <u>Daniel</u>

2. Write three Lesson 7 words that have only one syllable and have the /e/ sound.

   <u>dressed</u> <u>health</u>

   <u>death</u>

3. Write a Lesson 9 word in which /e/ is spelled **ay**. <u>says</u>

4. Write two Lesson 8 words that have only one syllable and have the /i/ sound.

   <u>shipped</u> <u>slipped</u>

5. Write two Lesson 8 words that have /i/ spelled **i** in more than one syllable.

   <u>minister</u> <u>finished</u>

6. Write two Lesson 8 words that have only one syllable and have /o/ spelled **o**.

   <u>dropped</u> <u>lock</u>

7. Write two Lesson 8 words that have /o/ spelled **a**.

   <u>watched</u> <u>wanted</u>

8. Write three Lesson 9 words that have only one syllable and have the /u/ sound.

   <u>blood</u> <u>rushed</u>

   <u>touch</u>

48

Review—Test Sentences

1.	*becomes*	Taking tests *becomes* a weekly habit.
2.	*wanted*	Zacchaeus *wanted* to see Jesus.
3.	*closed*	God *closed* the door of the ark.
4.	*blood*	Jesus shed His *blood* on the cross.
5.	*hello*	She called a cheery *hello* as I passed.
6.	*painting*	The men started *painting* the room.
7.	*invite*	Open the door and *invite* the guests in.
8.	*death*	Lazarus' *death* made Jesus sad.
9.	*reaches*	One person's influence *reaches* far.
10.	*grapes*	Grandma cooked *grapes* to make jelly.
11.	*country*	Japanese live in the *country* of Japan.
12.	*changing*	Jesus' first miracle was *changing* water to wine.

9. Write four Lesson 10 words that have the /ā/ sound but do not end with **day**.

_____raise_____ _____create_____

_____grapes_____ _____painting_____

10. Write three Lesson 10 words that have only one syllable and have the /ē/ sound.

_____cheese_____ _____preach_____

_____peace_____

11. Write six Lesson 11 words that have the /ī/ sound.

_____tried_____ _____shining_____

_____invite_____ _____tries_____

_____strike_____ _____climbed_____

12. Write two Lesson 11 words that have the /ō/ sound spelled **ow**.

_____throwing_____ _____bowl_____

13. Write the Lesson 11 words that have the /ō/ sound spelled **ew** or **oa**.

_____sewing_____ _____oatmeal_____

_____float_____

14. Write a Lesson 11 word that has /ō/ in the second syllable. _____hello_____

B. 13 points

B. Using Your Words Review

Fill in the puzzle with words that have the meanings given. Print one letter in each block, using capital letters. All the words are NEW WORDS in Lessons 7–11.

1. Abbreviation of the fourth day of the week.

2. Book of the Bible.

3. Want something that belongs to another.

4. Day of rest and worship.

5. Oats made into meal.

6. Completed.

7. First meal of the day.

8. Bible book that follows Psalms.

9. Soft covering.

10. Make from nothing.

11. Greeting.

12. Hollow, rounded dish.

13. Abbreviation of the first book of the Bible.

1. W E D.
2. E Z R A
3. C O V E T
4. S U N D A Y
5. O A T M E A L
6. F I N I S H E D
7. B R E A K F A S T
8. P R O V E R B S
9. B L A N K E T
10. C R E A T E
11. H E L L O
12. B O W L
13. G E N.

49

13. *created*   In six days God *created* everything.
14. *watched*   I *watched* for the mailman to come.
15. *cheese*   Slice some *cheese* for the sandwiches.
16. *tries*   Yes, the calf *tries* to walk but cannot.
17. *shopping*   Many customers were *shopping* early.
18. *begged*   A blind man sat and *begged*.
19. *punish*   God had to *punish* Achan for disobeying.
20. *minute*   "Just a *minute*," she said.
21. *ordered*   Mother *ordered* shoes from the catalog.
22. *shipped*   Grapefruits are *shipped* from Florida.
23. *climbed*   Green ivy *climbed* up the wall.
24. *float*   Did the axe head *float* or swim?
25. *sewing*   A man came to fix the *sewing* machine.
26. *throwing*   Try *throwing* the ball straight.

C. Building Words Review

C. 71 points

1. Here are some singular nouns. Write their plurals by adding **-s**, **-es**, or changing **y** to **i** before adding **-es**.

church _____churches_____

berry _____berries_____

chimney _____chimneys_____

minister _____ministers_____

flash _____flashes_____

2. Add **-ed** and **-ing** to each verb. You need to double the final consonant for some.

slip _____slipped_____ _____slipping_____

order _____ordered_____ _____ordering_____

beg _____begged_____ _____begging_____

ship _____shipped_____ _____shipping_____

print _____printed_____ _____printing_____

3. Add **-ed** and **-ing** to these verbs. Drop the final **e** in the root word.

create _____created_____ _____creating_____

raise _____raised_____ _____raising_____

close _____closed_____ _____closing_____

4. Add **-ed** and **-ing** to these verbs.

study _____studied_____ _____studying_____

try _____tried_____ _____trying_____

copy _____copied_____ _____copying_____

5. Add **-s** or **-es** to each verb.

float ____floats____ **reach** ____reaches____

6. Write the boldface words. Use slashes to divide the syllables by the pattern given.

a. VC/CV **invite** **breakfast**

_____in/vite_____ _____break/fast_____

b. VC/V **visit** **minute**

_____vis/it_____ _____min/ute_____

c. V/CV **papers** **sofa**

_____pa/pers_____ _____so/fa_____

7. Write these words. Put slashes between the syllables. If a consonant was doubled, divide between the consonants.

shopping   touches   shining   watches

_____shop/ping_____ _____shin/ing_____

_____touch/es_____ _____watch/es_____

8. Write the abbreviations for the underlined words.

Mister Newton Jones _____Mr._____

Mistress Lucy Derstine _____Mrs._____

Doctor Joel Martin _____Dr._____

Exodus 12:13 _____Ex._____

Daniel 1:8 _____Dan._____

2 Samuel 23:1 _____2 Sam._____

Numbers 23:19 _____Num._____

Proverbs 12:10 _____Prov._____

Judges 7:7 _____Judg._____

Esther 2:20 _____Esth._____

27. *tried*   Satan *tried* to get Jesus to sin.
28. *peace*   "Live in *peace*," Paul wrote.
29. *breakfast*   Cereal is a good *breakfast* food.
30. *wondered*   The lady *wondered* where to buy milk.
31. *touch*   You will burn your hand if you *touch* it.
32. *raise*   Farmers *raise* crops in the fields.
33. *Friday*   Her appointment is *Friday* morning.
34. *Thursday*   They have a meeting *Thursday* evening.
35. *Tuesday*   Each *Tuesday* the baker delivers bread.
36. *Esther*   Chapter 1 of *Esther* is about Vashti.
37. *Judges*   Chapter 1 of *Judges* is about Israel in Canaan.
38. *Numbers*   *Numbers* 1 tells of numbering Israel.
39. *2 Samuel*   We read of David's kingly life in *2 Samuel*.
40. *Joshua*   Chapter 1 of *Joshua* is about Joshua.

9. Write these references in a shorter way, using abbreviations and numerals. The first one is done as an example.

a. The Book of Romans, chapter thirteen, verse one. *Rom. 13:1*

b. The Book of Joshua, chapter one, verse nine. Josh. 1:9

c. The Book of Genesis, chapter two, verse seven. Gen. 2:7

d. The First Epistle to Timothy, chapter six, verse six. 1 Tim. 6:6

e. The Book of Numbers, chapter fifteen, verse forty-one. Num. 15:41

10. Write in order the names of the days of the week and their abbreviations.

Sunday	Sun.
Monday	Mon.
Tuesday	Tues.
Wednesday	Wed.
Thursday	Thur.
Friday	Fri.
Saturday	Sat.

Bible Thoughts

Use spelling words to complete these sentences.

11. A ___minister___ preaches the Gospel.

12. There will be no sorrow or suffering in ___heaven___.

13. God could ___create___ the world in six days.

14. "God is our refuge and strength, a very present help in ___trouble___." (Psalm 46:1).

51

41. *Genesis*   *Genesis* 1 is about the Creation.

For numbers 42–50, write *only* the abbreviations for the words.
42. *Dr.*   (Doctor)   He went to see *Dr.* Snyder.

For numbers 42–50, write only the abbreviations.
43. *Sat.*   (Saturday)   The day after Friday is *Saturday*.
44. *Thur.*   (Thursday)   The day after Wednesday is *Thursday*.
45. *Tues.*   (Tuesday)   The third day of the week is *Tuesday*.
46. *Sun.*   (Sunday)   The first day of the week is *Sunday*.

Remember, we are writing abbreviations.
47. *Gen.*   (Genesis)   The first book of the Bible is *Genesis*.
48. *2 Sam.*   (2 Samuel)   After 1 Samuel comes *2 Samuel*.
49. *Prov.*   (Proverbs)   After Psalms comes *Proverbs*.
50. *Esth.*   (Esther)   After Nehemiah comes *Esther*.

LESSON 13

NEW WORDS

few	mule
through	smooth
threw	tune
highway	goose
greatest	lowest
largest	finest
moonlight	sooner
schoolhouse	later

REVIEW WORDS

truth	flew
tooth	tomb

c/yōo/b

m/ōo/n

3. What letters spell /yōo/ in **cube**? ___u-e___

- Common spellings of the vowel sound /ōo/, as in **moon**, are **oo**, **u**, **o**, **u-e**, and **ew**. t**oo**th tr**u**th t**o** r**u**de fl**ew**

A. Sounds and Letters

- Common spellings of the vowel sound /yōo/, as in **cube**, are **u**, **u-e**, and **ew**. m**u**sic m**u**le f**ew**

1. The long sound of the letter **u** sounds exactly like the word **you** and is written like this: /yōo/. Write the spelling word that has /yōo/ spelled with the split digraph **u-e**. It will fit in this sentence.

   Absalom rode on a ___mule___.

2. Write the spelling word that has /yōo/ spelled **ew**. It will fit in this sentence.

   The boy had a ___few___ cents in his pocket.

4. In many words you hear the /ōo/ sound without /y/ before it. You hear the /ōo/ sound in all the REVIEW WORDS in this lesson. Write the REVIEW WORDS, and after them write the letters that spell /ōo/.

truth	u	flew	ew
tooth	oo	tomb	o

5. In which NEW WORDS does /ōo/ have these spellings?

   oo ___moonlight___   ___goose___
   ___schoolhouse___   ___sooner___
   ___smooth___   **ew** ___threw___
   ough ___through___

6. Some words may be pronounced with /ōo/ or /yōo/. For **dew**, some people say (dōo) and other people say (dyōo). Both are correct. **Tune** may be either (tōon) or (tyōon). Write **tune**. ___tune___ How is /ōo/ or /yōo/ spelled? ___u-e___

A. 30 points

52

Test Sentences

1. *few*	Jesus fed the people with only a *few* loaves.
2. *lowest*	The *lowest* line on the music staff is E.
3. *finest*	I used the pen with the *finest* point.
4. *highway*	A *highway* is named for Queen Elizabeth.
5. *largest*	The Pacific is the *largest* ocean.
6. *moonlight*	Leon ran by *moonlight* to the barn.
7. *schoolhouse*	He fixed the *schoolhouse* door.
8. *greatest*	"He that is *greatest* . . . shall be your servant."
9. *mule*	Listen to the *mule* braying.
10. *smooth*	Babine Lake is *smooth* in the morning.
11. *through*	In heaven, thieves do not break *through*.
12. *threw*	Kenneth *threw* away the wrapper.

7. Write spelling words to fit these clues.

a. /ā/ spelled **a** _____later_____

b. /ā/ spelled **ay** _____highway_____

c. /ā/ spelled **ea** _____greatest_____

d. /ī/ spelled **i** _____finest_____

e. /ō/ spelled **ow** _____lowest_____

f. /m/ spelled **mb** _____tomb_____

g. /ī/ spelled **igh**

_____highway_____   _____moonlight_____

h. final /s/ spelled **se**

_____schoolhouse_____   _____goose_____

B. Using Your Words

B. 23 points

Fill in the blanks with spelling words from the first column.

María and Pedro live on a mountainside in Guatemala. From their house, a winding footpath leads them to a main **(1)** _____highway_____. This path winds **(2)** _____through_____ a cornfield, past a **(3)** _____few_____ other houses, and through a creek in the valley. Five days a week, María and Pedro follow this two-mile path as they walk to their adobe-block **(4)** _____schoolhouse_____. They are thankful that they can go to a Christian school to learn the **(5)** _____truth_____ of God's Word.

6. Write two sentences of your own. Use **largest** and **schoolhouse** in the first sentence. Use **lowest** and **flew** in the second sentence.

a. _____(Individual sentences.)_____

b. _____

7. Write the correct homophones.

a. Joseph and Mary went (to, too, two) Bethlehem to pay their taxes. _____to_____

b. They could not stay in the inn because it was (to, too, two) full. _____too_____

c. The wise men went to Bethlehem (to, too, two). _____too_____

d. The wise men brought more than (to, too, two) gifts. _____two_____

e. The children of Israel walked (through, threw) the Red Sea. _____through_____

f. A poor widow (through, threw) two mites into the treasury. _____threw_____

53

13. *later*   It may be *later* than you think.
14. *tune*   We sang the same *tune* for both songs.
15. *sooner*   Kathy finished *sooner* than I did.
16. *goose*   The roast *goose* smells delicious.

From now on, I will not tell you anything about the end punctuation. You must decide yourself whether to use periods or question marks.

A *tooth* of the saw *flew* across the room.

The *truth* is that Jesus left the *tomb*.

g. Jonah preached as he walked (through, threw) Nineveh. _____through_____

8. Write spelling words that fit these clues.

a. A bird with a long neck. ___goose___

b. The musical sound of a song. ___tune___

c. Something we use to chew. ___tooth___

d. How birds got to the tree. ___flew___

--------- Interesting Words ---------

9. The way we pronounce some words is different from the way people pronounced them many years ago. Long ago people pronounced the **gh** in words such as **might** and **light**. Now we do not pronounce the **gh**. The way of saying **gh** words has changed, but the spelling has stayed the same.

Write three spelling words that have **gh**.

___through___   ___moonlight___

___highway___

C. Building Words

moon light

• **Compound Words**
A compound word is a word made by joining two words together. Most compound words are written with no space between the two smaller words.
   moon + light = moonlight
   high + way = highway

1. Write the two smaller words in each of the following compound words.

outdoors   ___out___   ___doors___

herself   ___her___   ___self___

storybook   ___story___   ___book___

toothache   ___tooth___   ___ache___

2. Find the compound words in the spelling list. Write them on the long lines. On the

short lines write the two smaller words that form each compound word.

___highway___   ___high___   ___way___

___moonlight___   ___moon___   ___light___

___schoolhouse___   ___school___   ___house___

• **Words That Compare**
To compare two things, add the suffix **-er** to an adjective or adverb.
   low + er = lower
   late + er = later
To compare three or more things, add the suffix **-est** to an adjective or adverb.
   low + est = lowest
   late + est = latest

C. 44 points

3. Use the suffixes **-er** and **-est** to compare these ropes.

The first rope is **strong**. The second rope is <u>stronger</u> than the first one. The third rope is the <u>strongest</u> of the three ropes.

4. Complete these sentences by using the bold-face words and their **-er** and **-est** forms.

a. **smooth**   Limestone feels <u>smooth</u>. Slate feels <u>smoother</u> than lime-stone. Marble feels the <u>smoothest</u> of the three rocks.

b. **old**   Adam grew to be an <u>old</u> man. Noah became even <u>older</u> than Adam. Methuselah was the <u>oldest</u> man who ever lived.

5. Write the **-er** and **-est** forms of these words. For some, you must drop the final **e** before adding the suffix.

soon	sooner	soonest
low	lower	lowest
fine	finer	finest

late	later	latest
great	greater	greatest
large	larger	largest

Dictionary Practice

6. Most dictionaries do not have an entry word for every form of a word. For example, you will usually not find **largest** as an entry word. You must look up **large**.

Suppose you want to find the meaning of each word below. Write the form that will be an entry word in a dictionary.

grapes	grape
changing	change
reaches	reach
created	create
copies	copy

Bible Thoughts

Use spelling words to complete these Bible verses.

7. Jesus said, "I am the way, the <u>truth</u>, and the life" (John 14:6).

8. "And an <u>highway</u> shall be there, and a way, and it shall be called The way of holiness" (Isaiah 35:8).

LESSON 14

NEW WORDS

stir
burnt
term
earlier
germs
earthworm
squirrel
curl

biggest
newspaper
sir
thinner
oldest
busiest
saddest
all right

REVIEW WORDS

birthday
hurry

early
world

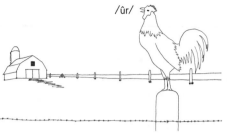

/ûr/

Discuss the various meanings of *all right*. Consider the sentence, "Your answers are all right."

A. Sounds and Letters

- The sound /ûr/, as in **bird**, is found only in accented syllables. Common spellings of /ûr/ are **er**, **ur**, **ir**, **or**, and **ear**.

    g**er**m c**ur**l b**ir**th w**or**ld **ear**ly

    After **w**, /ûr/ is usually spelled **or**.

    w<u>or</u>m   w<u>or</u>se

1. Write the one-syllable spelling words that have /ûr/ spelled **er**.

    term   _germs_

2. Write the one-syllable spelling words that have /ûr/ spelled **ur**.

    burnt   _curl_

3. Write the spelling words that have /ûr/ spelled **ir** (but not **irr**). _stir_

    sir   _birthday_

4. Write the spelling words that have /ûr/ spelled **or**.

    earthworm   _world_

5. Write the spelling words that have /ûr/ spelled **ear**. _earlier_

    earthworm   _early_

6. Write the two-syllable words that have /ûr/ spelled **irr** or **urr**.

    squirrel   _hurry_

7. The /ûr/ sound in each word should be spelled **ur**. Write the words correctly.

    b/ûr/n _burn_   h/ûr/t _hurt_

    t/ûr/n _turn_   ch/ûr/ch _church_

    pl/ûr/al _plural_   b/ûr/den _burden_

8. The /ûr/ sound in each word should be spelled **ir**. Write the words correctly.

    b/ûr/d _bird_   g/ûr/l _girl_

    f/ûr/m _firm_   d/ûr/t _dirt_

A. 38 points

56

Test Sentences

1.	*curl*	Their cat likes to *curl* up on the rug.
2.	*thinner*	Mervin used the *thinner* piece of wire.
3.	*saddest*	It was the *saddest* event in my life.
4.	*term*	The president serves a *term* of four years.
5.	*stir*	I must *stir* the pudding while it cooks.
6.	*earthworm*	An *earthworm* is a round worm.
7.	*newspaper*	The *newspaper* advertised a stove.
8.	*busiest*	Summer is the *busiest* season for them.
9.	*sir*	"Good evening, *sir*," the boy said.
10.	*germs*	Some *germs* cause diseases.
11.	*burnt*	The Jews gave *burnt* offerings to God.
12.	*biggest*	Rabbits ate the *biggest* plants.

9. Write the spelling words that have double consonants.

squirrel	saddest
biggest	all right
thinner	hurry

10. Which spelling words have the consonant blend **ld**?

oldest	world

B. Using Your Words

Write spelling words for these phonetic spellings.

11. jûrmz   germs

12. kûrl   curl

13. ûr′lē   early

14. nōōz′pā′ pər   newspaper

15. bûrth′dā′   birthday

16. biz′ē əst   busiest

B. 26 points

Fill in the blanks with spelling words from the first column.

This morning María is very excited. Today is her **(1)** ___birthday___ . She gets out of bed **(2)** ___earlier___ than usual to help her mother make tamales for a birthday treat. Mother has already collected corn leaves from the field. Now she and María cook the ground corn mixture and **(3)** ___stir___ it to keep it from getting **(4)** ___burnt___ . Next they wrap the mixture in the corn leaves and put these tamales into a pot to steam. A half hour later the tamales are finished. "Good-bye, Mother," María says. "I will give these to the neighbors and then **(5)** ___hurry___ to school." María's family has little to eat, but they know that God is pleased when they share what they do have.

6. Write two sentences of your own. Use **oldest** and **term** in the first sentence. Use **world** and **newspaper** in the second sentence.

a. _____(Individual sentences.)_____

b. _____

7. Write spelling words that fit these clues.

a. What we all live in. ___world___

b. What can run up a tree. ___squirrel___

c. What digs in the soil. ___earthworm___

d. What we can read. ___newspaper___

e. What can cause sickness. ___germs___

f. What your hair might do. ___curl___

g. What a school year is called. ___term___

57

13. *squirrel*   The *squirrel* moved swiftly.
14. *earlier*   Eugene came *earlier* than I did.
15. *oldest*   Methuselah was the *oldest* person.
16. *all right*   Donald is *all right* again.

Many in the *world* have a *birthday* today.

We must *hurry* to get to market *early*.

8. Write spelling words that are antonyms of the following words.

smallest _____biggest_____

youngest _____oldest_____

thicker _____thinner_____

late _____early_____

later _____earlier_____

happiest _____saddest_____

laziest _____busiest_____

madam _____sir_____

linger _____hurry_____

9. Which spelling word do people sometimes spell **alright**? ___all right___ **Remember: Alright** and **alwrong** are not correct. They are spelled **all right** and **all wrong**.

C. Building Words

C. 37 points

- **Compound Words**
  Some compound words are written as two separate words.
  post + office = post office

1. Which compound spelling word is written as two separate words? ___all right___

2. For each clue, write a compound word spelled as two words.

a. A **chair** for **rocking**.

_____rocking chair_____

b. A **skate** used on **ice**.

_____ice skate_____

c. A **storm** that brings much **dust**.

_____dust storm_____

d. A **lily** that grows in **water**.

_____water lily_____

e. A **plug** that makes a **spark**.

_____spark plug_____

3. Write spelling words for these meanings. Each is a compound written as one word.

a. A **paper** that tells the **news**.

_____newspaper_____

b. The **day** of one's **birth**.

_____birthday_____

c. A **worm** that digs in the **earth**.

_____earthworm_____

- **Words That Compare**
  In a one-syllable word having only one vowel and ending with a consonant, double the final consonant before adding **-er** or **-est**.   **hot + er = hotter**
                    hot + est = hottest

4. Write the **-er** and **-est** forms of the following words. Double the final consonant when necessary.

big   <u>bigger</u>   <u>biggest</u>

thin   <u>thinner</u>   <u>thinnest</u>

fast   <u>faster</u>   <u>fastest</u>

sad   <u>sadder</u>   <u>saddest</u>

5. When adding **-er** or **-est** to a word ending with a consonant and then **y**, you must change the <u>y</u> to <u>i</u>.

6. Write the **-er** and **-est** forms of these words.

early   <u>earlier</u>   <u>earliest</u>

busy   <u>busier</u>   <u>busiest</u>

easy   <u>easier</u>   <u>easiest</u>

Dictionary Practice

7. For each word below, write the form that will be an entry word in a dictionary.

thinnest <u>thin</u>

earlier <u>early</u>

germs <u>germ</u>

shining <u>shine</u>

8. At the top of each dictionary page are two boldface words called **guide words**. They show the first and last entry words on that page. Because entry words are in alphabetical order, you can tell from the guide words whether the word you are looking for is on that dictionary page.

Suppose you come to a dictionary page with the following guide words.

moon   **most**

Write whether each word below would be found **on**, **before**, or **after** that dictionary page.

moose <u>on</u>

mouse <u>after</u>

mop <u>on</u>

money <u>before</u>

mother <u>after</u>

morning <u>on</u>

Bible Thoughts

Use spelling words to complete these sentences.

9. In the Old Testament, God's people brought many <u>burnt</u> offerings to God (Leviticus 6:12).

10. The woman at Jacob's well said to Jesus, "<u>Sir</u>, thou hast nothing to draw with, and the well is deep: from whence then hast thou that living water?" (John 4:11).

LESSON 15

ch/âr/   p/âr/   /îr/   st/îr/   st/är/   b/är/n

NEW WORDS

prayer	friendly
heart	parents
their	everywhere
wears	truly
sharp	tear
slowly	somewhere
nearly	fairly
grandfather	grandpa

REVIEW WORDS

cheer	deer
share	pair

A. Sounds and Letters

> • In **chair** and **bear** we hear /âr/.
> Common spellings of /âr/ are **ar**,
> **are**, **air**, and **ear**.
>
> p**ar**ent   sh**are**   p**air**   w**ear**

1. Write the letters that spell /âr/ in each word below.

   chair ___air___   pear ___ear___

   various ___ar___   care ___are___

2. Complete the following sentences with spelling words in which /âr/ is spelled **ear** as in **pear**.

   a. Crease the paper first if you want to ___tear___ it straight.

   b. Father ___wears___ a hat.

3. One word that you just wrote may be pronounced in the following ways.

   a. (târ)   **b.** (tîr)

   Write the letter of the correct pronunciation for each meaning.

   _b_ A drop flowing from an eye.

   _a_ Pull apart; rip.

4. In which spelling words is /âr/ spelled **air**?

   ___fairly___   ___pair___

5. Write the NEW WORD in which /âr/ is spelled **ar** (not **are**). ___parents___

6. Write the REVIEW WORD in which /âr/ is spelled **are** at the end of the word.

   ___share___

7. One word with /âr/ spelled **ere** is **there**. A word that rhymes with **there** is in two spelling words. Write the two compound spelling words that have /âr/ spelled **ere**.

   ___everywhere___   ___somewhere___

   What **ere** word is in both words that you wrote? ___where___

A. 25 points

60

Test Sentences

1.	*parents*	Harold's *parents* love to sing.
2.	*somewhere*	God buried Moses *somewhere* in a valley.
3.	*everywhere*	Snow lay *everywhere* outdoors.
4.	*grandpa*	We plan to visit our *grandpa* soon.
5.	*heart*	A person's *heart* is the size of his fist.
6.	*prayer*	We end every *prayer* with "amen."
7.	*wears*	Mother *wears* a covering.
8.	*truly*	We are *truly* blessed by God.
9.	*friendly*	We must be *friendly* to have friends.
10.	*their*	The children recited *their* poems.
11.	*fairly*	Games played *fairly* are enjoyable.
12.	*slowly*	A car came *slowly* in the lane.

- Common spellings of /îr/, as in **deer**, are **ear** and **eer**.
  n<u>ear</u>   st<u>eer</u>

8. Fill in the blanks with spelling words that have /îr/ spelled **ear** as in the word **ear**.

   a. In heaven God shall wipe away every

   <u>   tear   </u> from our eyes.

   b. Digging the potatoes took <u> nearly </u>

   all afternoon.

9. In which spelling words is /îr/ spelled **eer** as in **steer**?

   <u>   cheer   </u> <u>   deer   </u>

B. Using Your Words

- The most common spelling of /är/, as in **star**, is **ar**.   **sh<u>ar</u>p   c<u>ar</u>t**

10. We hear /är/ in **star** and **barn**. Write the letters that spell /är/ in each word.

    star <u> ar </u>   barn <u> ar </u>

11. In which NEW WORD is /är/ spelled **ar** as in **star** and **barn**? <u>   sharp   </u>

Write spelling words for these phonetic spellings.

12. grand′pä′ <u>   grandpa   </u>

13. frend′lē <u>   friendly   </u>

14. trōō′lē <u>   truly   </u>

B. 26 points

Fill in the blanks with spelling words from the first column.

Today is Saturday, and Pedro is eager to help his **(1)** <u>grandfather</u> get the field ready for planting corn. Before leaving the house, Pedro gets the *azadón,* which is a large hoe. *Azadóns* are used by **(2)** <u> nearly </u> every farmer to dig up the soil because the countryside is much too hilly for tractors. Toward the end of the day, Grandfather and Pedro work more **(3)** <u> slowly </u>. Hoeing is hard work, and **(4)** <u> their </u> backs become tired. Before Pedro returns home, Grandfather says, "I appreciate your willingness to **(5)** <u> share </u> in the work."

6. Write two sentences of your own. Use **parents** and **fairly** in the first sentence. Use **nearly** and **sharp** in the second sentence.

   a. <u>   (Individual sentences.)   </u>

   b. <u>   </u>

61

13. *tear*   A *tear* slid down her cheek.
14. *grandfather*   His *grandfather* has gray hair.
15. *sharp*   Carry a *sharp* knife with the point down.
16. *nearly*   The sun shone *nearly* all day.

I ate my *share* of the *deer* meat.

A *pair* of new boots may *cheer* the poor man.

7. Homophones are words that sound alike but are spelled differently. Write the spelling words that are homophones of these words.

hart ____heart____   dear ____deer____

tare ____tear____   pare ____pair____

there ____their____

8. Complete these sentences with the words you wrote above.

a. You could not live without a __heart__.

b. A lion can ____tear____ a giraffe into pieces.

c. Joseph and Mary offered a ____pair____ of turtledoves for Jesus.

d. The books belonging to them are ____their____ books.

e. A hart is a male ____deer____.

C. Building Words

Compound Words

1. Which compound NEW WORDS end alike?

____everywhere____   ____somewhere____

2. Build other words by joining **every** to **body**, **one**, and **thing**.   ____everybody____

____everyone____   ____everything____

3. Join **some** to **body**, **one**, and **thing**.

9. Complete the following sentences with spelling words.

a. Let us go to the nursing home and ____cheer____ the old people.

b. A child without ____parents____ is an orphan.

c. A godly person ____wears____ modest clothing.

d. Jesus spent many hours in ____prayer____ to His heavenly Father.

10. Which NEW WORDS mean "the father of one's father or mother"?

____grandfather____   ____grandpa____

11. Which spelling word can be used in place of **father and mother**?

____parents____

____somebody____   ____someone____

____something____

4. Join **any** to **one** and **thing**.

____anyone____   ____anything____

5. Build compound words by joining each word in the first column to a word in the second column.

C. 32 points

up	port	upstairs
air	beat	airport
basket	stairs	basketball
rein	ball	reindeer
heart	deer	heartbeat

6. Which compound spelling words begin with the same word?

__grandfather__   __grandpa__

Join that same beginning to another spelling word to name these people.

__grandparents__

7. Build words by joining **grand** to **mother** and **ma**.

__grandmother__   __grandma__

• **The -ly Suffix**
  Adding **-ly** to some words changes them to adverbs.
  kind + ly = kindly This adverb means "in a kind manner."

Write spelling words that have the following meanings.

8. In a slow manner. __slowly__

9. In the manner of a friend. __friendly__

10. In a fair manner. __fairly__

11. In a true manner. __truly__

12. Add **-ly** to a word from the first sentence to form an adverb that completes the second sentence.

  a. We are near to our home. We are __nearly__ home.

  b. The prophet gave a sharp rebuke. He spoke __sharply__.

  c. Karen is glad she can work. She works __gladly__.

13. Which spelling word is a form of **true**? __truly__ Which letter in **true** was dropped to add **-ly**? __e__

Bible Thoughts

Use spelling words to complete these Bible verses.

14. "A man that hath friends must shew himself __friendly__: and there is a friend that sticketh closer than a brother" (Proverbs 18:24).

15. "Lying lips are abomination to the LORD: but they that deal __truly__ are his delight" (Proverbs 12:22).

16. "Jesus . . . said unto the sick of the palsy; Son, be of good __cheer__; thy sins be forgiven thee" (Matthew 9:2).

LESSON 16

NEW WORDS

turtle	temple
evil	needle
bottle	marbles
animals	idol
travel	buckle
rainy	angel
healthy	muddy
gentle	angry

REVIEW WORDS

middle	pencil
dirty	handle

ol   al   le   il

hand/əl/   el

A. Sounds and Letters

- The most common spelling of /əl/ in an unaccented syllable at the end of a word is **le**.   **temp<u>le</u>**
  Other spellings of /əl/ are **el**, **il**, **al**, and **ol**.
  ang<u>el</u> penc<u>il</u> anim<u>al</u> car<u>ol</u>

1. Write the spelling words in which /əl/ is
spelled **le**.   turtle

____bottle____   ____marbles____

____gentle____   ____buckle____

____temple____   ____middle____

____needle____   ____handle____

2. Make other words by adding **le** to each word
below. The first answer is **pickle**.

pick ___pickle___   beet ___beetle___

crack ___crackle___   steep ___steeple___

3. Write the spelling words in which /əl/ is
spelled the same as in the words shown.

bushel   ____travel____   ____angel____

pupil   ____evil____   ____pencil____

royal   ___animals___

carol   ____idol____

4. Write the spelling words that have double
consonants. Put slashes between the double
consonants to divide them into syllables,
like this: **pud/dle**.   ____bot/tle____

____mud/dy____   ____mid/dle____

5. Which NEW WORD has both **m** and **n**?

_____animals_____

Which letter comes first, **m** or **n**? ___n___

6. Which NEW WORD has /e/ spelled **ea**?

_____healthy_____

A. 39 points

64

Test Sentences

1.	*temple*	A Christian's body is the *temple* of God.
2.	*needle*	Did you find Aunt Mary's *needle* for her?
3.	*buckle*	Carl helped Philip to *buckle* his boots.
4.	*travel*	I hope to *travel* to another state.
5.	*gentle*	Our pony is a *gentle* animal.
6.	*healthy*	Thank God for a *healthy* body.
7.	*turtle*	A box *turtle* can make a good pet.
8.	*angry*	Do not be *angry* with others.
9.	*animals*	Many *animals* went into the ark.
10.	*rainy*	We have had much *rainy* weather.
11.	*evil*	Every person is born with an *evil* nature.
12.	*bottle*	The milk *bottle* is nearly empty.

7. Write the spelling word that has

/ûr/ spelled **ir**. _____dirty_____

/ûr/ spelled **ur**. _____turtle_____

8. Write the NEW WORD that

begins like **raise**. _____rainy_____

ends with **gry**. _____angry_____

Write spelling words for these phonetic spellings. On the second line, write how many syllables the word has.

9. hel'thē _____healthy_____ __2__

10. dûr'tē _____dirty_____ __2__

11. an'ə məlz _____animals_____ __3__

12. ang'grē _____angry_____ __2__

13. rā'nē _____rainy_____ __2__

B. Using Your Words

B. 26 points

Fill in the blanks with spelling words from the first column.

It is nearing the month of May. The six months of dry season are coming to an end. Both María and Pedro know that the **(1)** _____rainy_____ season is about to begin. Now for the next six months it will rain nearly every day. Even in the rainy season, the forenoon can be clear and sunny. But then about the **(2)** _____middle_____ of the day, clouds begin to form; and soon María and Pedro hear the **(3)** _____gentle_____ pitter-patter of rain. Sometimes they get caught in the rain as they bring the **(4)** _____animals_____ home from the grazing spot. To stay dry, the children cover themselves with large sheets of plastic. Of course, their bare feet still get **(5)** _____dirty_____ as they hurry along the muddy path.

6. Write two sentences of your own. Use **turtle** and **travel** in the first sentence. Use **marbles** and **dirty** in the second sentence.

a. _____(Individual sentences.)_____

b. _____

7. Some words can have two meanings. Write the same spelling word in both blanks of each sentence below.

a. Mother will _____bottle_____ the milk and give the _____bottle_____ to the baby.

b. Please sharpen this _____pencil_____ and then _____pencil_____ the design with it.

65

13. *muddy*   The hurricane left *muddy* water everywhere.

14. *marbles*   The *marbles* rolled across the floor.

15. *angel*   God sent an *angel* to help Daniel.

16. *idol*   Aaron disobeyed and made an *idol* of gold.

Handle the *pencil* with care.

Who put *dirty* marks in the *middle* of the hall?

c. The ___buckle___ on Edwin's boot was broken, so he could no longer ___buckle___ it.

d. Father said we should not ___handle___ the teacup, because he had just finished gluing the broken ___handle___ .

e. Because of fast ___travel___ , people of today can ___travel___ to faraway places in a short time.

C. Building Words

rain y   mud d y   tur tle   pick le

- **The -y Suffix**
  Adding **-y** to some nouns can change them to adjectives.
  Putting **salt** into water makes **salty** water (water having salt).

1. Write a spelling word for each meaning.

   a. Having good health. ___healthy___

   b. Having rain. ___rainy___

   c. Having dirt on it. ___dirty___

   d. Having mud on it. ___muddy___

2. Look at the words you wrote for number 1. In which word was the final consonant doubled before adding **-y**? ___muddy___

3. Build words by adding **-y** to the boldface words.

   a. **cloud** The sky is ___cloudy___ today.

   b. **wind** Kites are for ___windy___ days.

8. Write the spelling words that these words make you think of.

   a. bad, wicked ___evil___

   b. journey, car ___travel___

   c. Baal, Dagon ___idol___

   d. Gabriel, messenger ___angel___

   e. write, wooden ___pencil___

   f. shell, slow ___turtle___

   g. sew, thread ___needle___

   c. **sand** This field has ___sandy___ soil.

   d. **cheer** Sue had a ___cheery___ smile.

   e. **pearl** Heaven has ___pearly___ gates.

4. Build words as in number 3. Double the final consonants in these words.

   a. **sun** It was a warm, ___sunny___ day.

   b. **star** God made the ___starry___ skies.

   c. **fog** London has much ___foggy___ weather.

   d. **knot** This wood is very ___knotty___ .

   e. **fur** A rabbit has a ___furry___ coat.

5. What spelling word means "feeling or showing anger"? ___angry___

   What letter is in **anger** that is not in the word you wrote? ___e___

C. 38 points

• **Syllables**
When a word ends with **le**, the consonant before the **le** usually joins the **le** to form the last syllable.   **tur/tle   nee/dle**

6. Write the spelling words that end with **le**. (Include the plural word but not **buckle**.) Put slashes between the syllables.

tur/tle	nee/dle
bot/tle	mar/bles
gen/tle	mid/dle
tem/ple	han/dle

• The letters **ck** form a digraph that must not be divided. When **ck** comes before **le**, divide between **ck** and **le**.   **pick/le   chuck/le**

7. Write the spelling word that has the digraph **ck** and ends with **le**. Put a slash between the syllables.

buck/le

8. Use slashes to divide these words into syllables according to the rule above.

cack/le   sick/le   freck/le
trick/le   speck/le   knuck/le

9. When **ng** or **nk** comes before the final **le**, the syllable division comes after the **n**: **tan/gle, twin/kle**. Use this rule to divide the following words.

ju n/g l e   si n/g l e   wri n/k l e

Bible Thoughts

Use spelling words to complete these sentences.

10. The Bible tells us that the Christian's body is the _____temple_____ of the Holy Ghost (1 Corinthians 6:19).

11. "The _____angel_____ of the LORD encampeth round about them that fear him, and delivereth them" (Psalm 34:7).

12. Balaam was _____angry_____ with his donkey (Numbers 22:27).

LESSON 17

NEW WORDS

cousin
robin
often
person
ocean
happened
ribbon
lessons

fifth
fifteenth
ninety
nineteen
eighty
eighteen
thirteen
seventeen

REVIEW WORDS

cotton
seven

sixty
thirty

A. Sounds and Letters

- The most common spelling of the /ən/ or /in/ ending is **en**. sev**en**
  Other spellings of final /ən/ or /in/ are **on** and **in**.
  pers**on**   rob**in**

1. In many of the spelling words, you hear /ən/ or /in/ at the end of the word or its root word. Write the spelling words in which final /ən/ or /in/ is spelled the same as in

   a. op**en**   ___often___   ___seventeen___
   ___happened___   ___seven___

doz/ən/

on   in   en

b. mel**on**   ___person___   ___lessons___
___ribbon___   ___cotton___

c. cab**in**   ___cousin___   ___robin___

2. In each word that you wrote for number 1, the /ən/ or /in/ ending is in a syllable that is (accented, <u>unaccented</u>).

3. Which NEW WORD in the second column ended with /ən/ before the suffix **-teen** was added?   ___seventeen___

4. The /ən/ sound in each word below should be spelled **en**. Write the words correctly.

   doz/ən/   ___dozen___   sudd/ən/   ___sudden___
   lin/ən/   ___linen___   gold/ən/   ___golden___
   eat/ən/   ___eaten___   heath/ən/   ___heathen___
   rav/ən/   ___raven___   kitch/ən/   ___kitchen___

5. The /ən/ sound in each word should be spelled **on**. Write the words correctly.

   apr/ən/   ___apron___   butt/ən/   ___button___
   li/ən/   ___lion___   reas/ən/   ___reason___

6. Which NEW WORD starts with /ō/?

   ___ocean___   If /sh/ in this word is spelled **ce**, how is /ən/ spelled?   ___an___

A. 38 points

68

Test Sentences

1. *robin*   In the spring the *robin* flies north.
2. *ocean*   The waters of the *ocean* never stop moving.
3. *lessons*   The Bible has many *lessons* for us.
4. *eighteen*   We will buy *eighteen* oranges.
5. *ninety*   Not many people live *ninety* years.
6. *ribbon*   The Jews wore a blue *ribbon* on their garments.
7. *person*   One other *person* works there.
8. *nineteen*   Rebecca is *nineteen* years old.
9. *seventeen* Ernest has *seventeen* rabbits.
10. *fifth*   What did God make on the *fifth* day?
11. *cousin*   My aunt and my *cousin* made cookies.
12. *eighty*   Did you read *eighty* pages?

7. The /ən/ sound in each word below should be spelled **an**. Write the words correctly.

org/ən/ ___organ___   Americ/ən/ ___American___

8. Write **ninety**. _____ninety_____ What split digraph spells /ī/? ___i-e___ Which other spelling word has /ī/ spelled like /ī/ in **ninety**? _____nineteen_____

Write spelling words for these phonetic spellings.

9. ā′tē _____eighty_____

10. pûr′sən _____person_____

11. thûr tēn′ _____thirteen_____

12. fif tēnth′ _____fifteenth_____

13. kot′ən _____cotton_____

14. ō′shən _____ocean_____

15. ô′fən _____often_____

B. Using Your Words

B. 25 points

Fill in the blanks with spelling words from the first column.

Mother, Father, María, and Pedro are on a special bus trip. They are leaving the mountains to visit Uncle René, Aunt Marta, and Elsa, who is María and Pedro's **(1)** ___cousin___. Uncle René's family lives near the **(2)** ___ocean___, so the children do not see each other **(3)** ___often___. The winding road down the mountain reminds María of a tangled **(4)** ___ribbon___. Each mile downward the air becomes warmer. Up where María and Pedro live, the climate is cool, and wheat and corn are grown. At the coast where Elsa lives, it is warm enough to raise **(5)** ___cotton___.

6. Write two sentences of your own. Use **seven** and **robin** in the first sentence. Use **cousin** and **person** in the second sentence.

a. _____(Individual sentences.)_____

b. _____

7. Fill in the blanks with spelling words.

a. **Cookbook** is to **recipes** as **textbook** is to _____lessons_____.

b. **Scale** is to **goldfish** as **feather** is to _____robin_____.

13. *happened*   The accident *happened* around noon.
14. *thirteen*   Uncle Abram milks *thirteen* cows.
15. *often*   We thank our parents *often* for their care.
16. *fifteenth*   It suits on the *fifteenth* of May.

Mary made *cotton* dresses for her *seven* girls.

Had he wanted *thirty* or *sixty* chairs?

c. **Lassie** is to **dog** as **Wayne** is to

_____person_____ .

d. **Undone** is to **unfinished** as **occurred** is

to _____happened_____ .

e. **Car** is to **land** as **ship** is to __ocean__ .

8. Write the missing numbers.

a. ten, twenty, ___thirty___ , forty, fifty,

___sixty___ , seventy, ___eighty___ ,

___ninety___ , one hundred

b. eleven, twelve, ___thirteen___ , fourteen,

fifteen, sixteen, ___seventeen___ ,

___eighteen___ , ___nineteen___

c. We will have a song service on the

___fifth___ Sunday of the month.

d. When we reach the ___fifteenth___ day of

April, the month will be half gone.

e. Mabel was ___seven___ years old when

she started school.

C. Building Words

C. 43 points

• **The -teen, -ty, and -th Suffixes**
three + teen or ty: Change three
   to thir.   thirteen   thirty
four + ty: Drop the u.   forty
five + teen, ty, or th: Change ve
   to f.   fifteen   fifty   fifth
eight + teen, ty, or th: Use only
   one t.   eighteen eighty eighth

1. Build other number names by adding **-teen**
and **-ty** to the names below.

six   ___sixteen___   ___sixty___

seven   ___seventeen___   ___seventy___

nine   ___nineteen___   ___ninety___

2. Add **-teen** and **-ty** to **four**. You will drop

the letter _u_ in the second word.

___fourteen___   ___forty___

3. Add **-teen** and **-ty** to **eight**. Use only one **t**.

___eighteen___   ___eighty___

4. Add **-teen** and **-ty** to **three**. First change
three to **thir**.

___thirteen___   ___thirty___

5. Add **-teen** and **-ty** to **five**. Change **ve** to **f**.

___fifteen___   ___fifty___

6. The suffix **-th** can be added to build words
that tell "which one." Complete this sentence with NEW WORDS that end with **th** and
tell "which one."

Ann lived in house number fifteen on

street number five, so she lived in the

___fifteenth___ house on the ___fifth___

street.

7. Use the suffix **-th** to build other words that tell "which one."

four ___fourth___   six ___sixth___

seven ___seventh___   ten ___tenth___

• **Syllables**
Compound words are divided into syllables between the two smaller words.   **moon/light**
If a suffix adds a syllable to a word, divide between the root word and the suffix.   **lat/est**

---

8. Divide these compound words into syllables.

high/way   school/house

rain/bow   grand/pa

9. Divide these into syllables between the root words and the suffixes.

near/ly   larg/est

nine/teen   friend/ly

great/er   soon/er

10. Decide whether the suffix of each word is **-ty** or just **-y.** Then write the root word.

hearty ___heart___   loyalty ___loyal___

ninety ___nine___   trusty ___trust___

11. In some of these words, the **-ty** is a suffix. In others, the **t** is part of the root word and suffix is just **-y.** Divide them into syllables between the root words and the suffixes.

for/ty   thir/ty

sal t/y   dir t/y

dus t/y   seven/ty

Bible Thoughts

Use spelling words to complete these sentences.

12. God created the fish and birds on the ___fifth___ day (Genesis 1:20–23).

13. God made the week to be ___seven___ days long.

LESSON 18

13	14	15	16	17
few	sir	prayer	turtle	cousin
through	burnt	heart	evil	robin
threw	term	their	bottle	often
highway	earlier	wears	animals	person
greatest	germs	sharp	travel	ocean
largest	earthworm	slowly	rainy	happened
moonlight	squirrel	nearly	healthy	ribbon
schoolhouse	curl	grandfather	gentle	lessons
mule	biggest	friendly	temple	fifth
smooth	newspaper	parents	needle	fifteenth
tune	stir	everywhere	marbles	ninety
goose	thinner	truly	idol	nineteen
lowest	oldest	tear	buckle	eighty
finest	busiest	somewhere	angel	eighteen
sooner	saddest	fairly	muddy	thirteen
later	all right	grandpa	angry	seventeen

A. Sounds and Letters Review

A. 66 points

1. At the beginning of each group of words, you see the symbol for the missing vowel sound. Fill in the blanks with the correct letters.

/a/ gr_a_ndpa   _a_nimals   /ā/ _a_ngel l_a_t_e_ r_ai_ny   highw_ay_

/e/ l_e_ssons h_ea_lthy   /ē/ _e_vil n_ee_dle r_ea_ch angr_y_

/i/ f_i_fth r_i_bbon   /ī/ _i_dol n_i_n_e_ all r_igh_t tr_y_

/o/ b_o_ttle w_a_tch   /ō/ _o_ld cl_o_s_e_ fl_oa_t sl_ow_

/u/ b_u_ckle s_o_me   /yo͞o/ or /o͞o/ m_u_l_e_ f_ew_ t_oo_th

c_ou_sin bl_oo_d

2. Write **earthworm**. _earthworm_
What letters spell /ûr/ after **w**? _or_

3. Write **friendly**. _friendly_
What letters spell /e/? _ie_

4. Write **eighty** and the four letters that spell /ā/. _eighty_ _eigh_
Then write **greatest** and the two letters that spell /ā/. _greatest_ _ea_

72

Review—Test Sentences

1. *later* — Sooner or *later* it will rain again.
2. *schoolhouse* — The *schoolhouse* was warm.
3. *few* — "The harvest truly is great, but the labourers are *few*."
4. *sir* — I'm sorry, *sir,* but Father is not here.
5. *nearly* — Your lunch boxes are *nearly* alike.
6. *sooner* — Should we start *sooner* than two o'clock?
7. *person* — The first *person* God created was Adam.
8. *often* — Thank God *often* for a sound mind.
9. *largest* — Asia is the *largest* continent.
10. *tune* — I thought the *tune* sounded familiar.
11. *highway* — Bartimaeus sat by the *highway* begging.
12. *earthworm* — A robin ate the *earthworm* quickly.

For numbers 5–11, you see outlines of animals whose names have the sounds you studied. Fill in the blanks with NEW WORDS that have various spellings of those sounds.

5. g/o͞o/se, tr/o͞o/ly, sm/o͞o/th, n/o͞o/spaper, t/o͞o/ne

goose	newspaper
truly	tune
smooth	

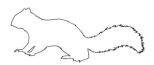

6. squ/ûr/el, /ûr/thw/ûr/m, b/ûr/nt, t/ûr/m

| squirrel | burnt |
| earthworm | term |

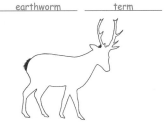

7. m/är/bles, h/är/t

| marbles | heart |

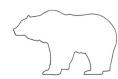

8. p/âr/ents, f/âr/ly, w/âr/s, pr/âr/, everywh/âr/

parents	prayer
fairly	everywhere
wears	

9. n/îr/ly, t/îr/

| nearly | tear |

10. turt/əl/, trav/əl/, ev/əl/, anim/əl/s, id/əl/

turtle	animals
travel	idol
evil	

11. rob/in/, ribb/ən/, oft/ən/, oce/ən/

| robin | often |
| ribbon | ocean |

73

13. *newspaper* — Put the *newspaper* on the pile.
14. *everywhere* — Weeds grew *everywhere* we looked.
15. *marbles* — Two *marbles* rolled under the sofa.
16. *animals* — God created all the *animals*.
17. *eighty* — Mother picked *eighty* quarts of berries.
18. *travel* — Wild geese *travel* many miles.
19. *muddy* — Wipe off your *muddy* shoes.
20. *smooth* — Naaman's new flesh was soft and *smooth*.
21. *temple* — The *temple* was a place of worship.
22. *saddest* — The dog had the *saddest*-looking eyes.
23. *burnt* — Forest fires have *burnt* many trees.
24. *ninety* — Who is over *ninety* years old?
25. *seventeen* — Joseph was *seventeen* when he was sold.

B. Using Your Words Review

B. 29 points

Fill in the crossword puzzle with NEW WORDS from Lessons 13–17. Use all capital letters.

Across

1. Small colored balls.   marbles
4. After the usual time.   later
7. Bird that is like a duck but is larger and has a longer neck.   goose
8. Bad.   evil
9. Music.   tune
10. Tossed; hurled.   threw
11. Having a good cutting edge.   sharp
13. Publication telling the news.   newspaper
16. Mild; not severe or rough.   gentle
20. At all places.   everywhere
21. Title of respect for a man.   sir
22. Most excellent; best.   finest
23. Unhappiest; most sorrowful.   saddest

Down

2. Messenger from God.   angel
3. Earlier.   sooner
4. Things to be learned.   lessons
5. Having many showers.   rainy
6. Next after the fourteenth.   fifteenth
10. Three more than ten.   thirteen
12. Took place; occurred.   happened
14. Biggest; largest.   greatest
15. Nearest to the ground.   lowest
17. Reptile with a hard shell.   turtle
18. Not many.   few
19. Has on for clothing.   wears

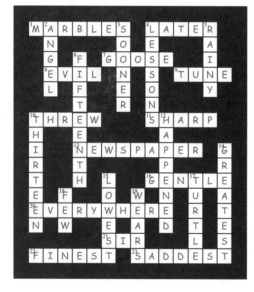

74

26. *mule*   The *mule* likes grass and oats.
27. *grandpa*   Ask your *grandpa* which he wants.
28. *fairly*   This book is *fairly* new.
29. *ocean*   The ship crossed the *ocean* in five days.
30. *lowest*   We could reach the two *lowest* branches.
31. *lessons*   I finished my *lessons* early.
32. *their*   Our neighbors lost *their* dog.
33. *heart*   God knows the secrets of each *heart*.
34. *goose*   A *goose* has webbed feet.
35. *wears*   Grandpa *wears* glasses only to read.
36. *all right*   That is *all right* with me.
37. *parents*   "Obey your *parents* in the Lord."
38. *evil*   "Deliver us from *evil*," we pray.

Write spelling words for these phonetic spellings.

24. skwûr′əl _____squirrel_____

25. nîr′lē _____nearly_____

26. ān′jəl _____angel_____

27. kuz′in _____cousin_____

C. Building Words Review

1. Complete each phrase by adding **-er** to the boldface word. Double the consonant, drop the **e**, or change the **y** to **i** if needed.

   smooth ___smoother___ than glass

   thin ___thinner___ than paper

   busy ___busier___ than a bee

   fine ___finer___ than sand

2. Complete each phrase by adding **-est** to the boldface word. Make changes in the root words if needed.

   great the ___greatest___ event

   late the ___latest___ news

   early the ___earliest___ flowers

   sad the ___saddest___ day

3. Build words by combining these root words and suffixes. Make changes in the root words if needed.

   slow + ly = _____slowly_____

   true + ly = _____truly_____

   health + y = _____healthy_____

   mud + y = _____muddy_____

nine + teen = _____nineteen_____

eight + teen = _____eighteen_____

fifteen + th = _____fifteenth_____

five + th = _____fifth_____

nine + ty = _____ninety_____

eight + ty = _____eighty_____

4. Divide each word into syllables between the root word and the suffix.

   s o o n/e r   l o w/l y   f r i e n d/l y
   f i n/e s t   m u d/d y   s h i n/i n g
   n o d/d e d   f r y/i n g   b u r n/i n g
   b i g/g e s t   d r i/e r   p r e a c h/e s

5. Divide each word into syllables. Keep a consonant with **le** unless it follows **ck**.

   t e m/p l e   g e n/t l e
   b u c k/l e   n e e/d l e

6. Write the compound word that means

   a. light from the moon. ___moonlight___

   b. a house for school. ___schoolhouse___

Bible Thoughts

Complete these verses with spelling words from Lesson 16.

7. "But we were ___gentle___ among you, even as a nurse cherisheth her children" (1 Thessolonians 2:7).

8. "It is easier for a camel to go through the eye of a _____needle_____, than for a rich man to enter into the kingdom of God" (Matthew 19:24).

C. 38 points

75

39. *prayer* God heard the *prayer* of the widow.
40. *through* Jonah walked *through* Nineveh, preaching.
41. *needle* Can you thread the *needle* yourself?
42. *cousin* He has no *cousin* near his age.
43. *healthy* Working outdoors is *healthy* exercise.
44. *fifteenth* They came on the *fifteenth* of May.
45. *term* The school *term* is half over.
46. *squirrel* Now the *squirrel* can eat his nuts.
47. *earlier* If he knocked *earlier,* I did not hear.
48. *idol* How sad to pray to an *idol* for rain.
49. *busiest* Friday is the *busiest* day of the week.
50. *thinner* Onionskin paper is *thinner* than this.

LESSON 19

NEW WORDS

Mennonite Trinity
arithmetic balloon
supply company
among enemy
preacher holiday
teacher's interesting
grandma's sugar
surprise different

REVIEW WORDS

driver thousand
cellar colors

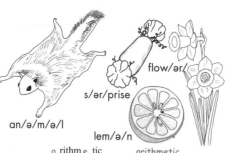

flow/ər/

s/ər/prise

an/ə/m/ə/l

lem/ə/n

_a_ rithm _e_ tic _____ arithmetic _____

en _e_ my _____ enemy _____

hol _i_ day _____ holiday _____

Trin _i_ ty _____ Trinity _____

Menn _o_ nite _____ Mennonite _____

s _u_ pply _____ supply _____

> • When /ə/ is the only sound in the first syllable of a word, /ə/ is usually spelled **a**. **along among**

2. What two spelling words begin with /ə/?

_____ arithmetic _____ among

> • The sound /ər/ is found only in unaccented syllables. **hamm_er_**
> The most·common spelling of /ər/ is **er**. Other spellings of /ər/ are **or**, **ar**, and **ur**. **cov_er_ col_or_ sug_ar_ sulf_ur_**

3. Remember that /ər/ is found only in unaccented syllables. Write the spelling words in which /ər/ is spelled like

a. /ər/ in **other**. _____ interesting

_____ preacher _____ different

_____ teacher's _____ driver

A. 40 points

A. Sounds and Letters

> • The vowel sound in many unaccented syllables is /ə/, as in **b_a_n_a_n_a_**. Common spellings of /ə/ are **a**, **e**, **o**, and **u**. **sof_a_ ev_e_n ribb_o_n loc_u_st**

> • In some unaccented syllables, /i/ or /ə/ is spelled **i**. **Trin_i_ty**

1. In each spelling word below, print the letter that spells /ə/ or /i/. Then write the word.

comp _a_ ny _____ company _____

_a_ mong _____ among _____

b _a_ lloon _____ balloon _____

76

Test Sentences

1.	*preacher*	Noah was a *preacher* of righteousness.
2.	*supply*	"But my God shall *supply* all your need."
3.	*company*	Jesus fed a great *company* of people.
4.	*enemy*	Our *enemy* Satan wants us to do bad things.
5.	*Trinity*	In the *Trinity* there are three persons.
6.	*Mennonite*	The *Mennonite* people obeyed God.
7.	*among*	Divide the apples *among* the three girls.
8.	*surprise*	Did the sun *surprise* you?
9.	*balloon*	A toy *balloon* stretches.
10.	*different*	A wasp is *different* from a bee.
11.	*interesting*	How *interesting* to watch ants!
12.	*sugar*	Much *sugar* comes from sugar cane.

b. /ər/ in **doctor**.   colors

c. /ər/ in **murmur**.   surprise

d. /ər/ in **dollar**.   sugar

          cellar

Write spelling words for these phonetic spellings.

5. prē'chər   preacher

6. shoͦog'ər   sugar

7. ə mung'   among

8. bə loͦon'   balloon

9. dif'ər ənt   different

4. Write the spelling words that have double

consonants.   Mennonite

          supply   different

          balloon   cellar

B. Using Your Words

B. 27 points

Fill in the blanks with spelling words from the first column.

   "Let us do good unto all men, especially unto them who are of the household of faith"

(Galatians 6:10). The Millers were on their way to visit Grandma. Since she was not

expecting them, it would be a **(1)**   surprise . Before long they arrived at Grandma's

house, which was next to the Riverside **(2)**   Mennonite   Church. Grandma lived

alone. Lloyd and Luke decided to bring in a **(3)**   supply   of wood and stack it in

the **(4)**   cellar   They knew this would please her. Their **(5)**   grandma's   hearty

"thank you" kept ringing in their ears on the way home.

6. Write two sentences of your own. Use **teacher's** and **arithmetic** in the first sentence. Use **different** and **driver** in the second sentence.

   a.   (Individual sentences.)

   b.

Which spelling words fit these definitions?

7. Group of people.   company

8. Vacation.   holiday

9. In the midst of.   among

10. Not a friend.   enemy

11. Something sweet made from cane.

          sugar

77

13. *holiday*   A Thanksgiving *holiday* is once a year.
14. *arithmetic*   In *arithmetic* we add numbers.
15. *grandma's*   Amy saw her *grandma's* old chest.
16. *teacher's*   The *teacher's* helpers are cleaning.

The *driver* loads boxes of many *colors*.

One *thousand* jars were in the *cellar*.

12. Father, Son, and Holy Spirit.

_____Trinity_____

13. Catch unprepared. _____surprise_____

14. Holding one's attention.

_____interesting_____

15. Mathematics. _____arithmetic_____

16. Not the same _____different_____

17. Do not confuse **colors** and **collars**. Red, yellow, blue, and green are ___colors___. Shirt or dress parts that go around the neck are ___collars___.

18. Write **colors** or **collars** in each blank.

a. What ___colors___ are in the rainbow?

b. Four-year-old Alma knows the names of many ___colors___.

c. Mother straightened the twisted ___collars___ on several shirts.

d. How many ___colors___ of paint do you need?

e. Making ___collars___ for these dresses is hard.

f. Some shirt ___collars___ are held down by small buttons.

C. Building Words

C. 21 points

• **The -er Suffix**
Adding **-er** to some words makes them nouns by naming "one who does." A person who **farms** is a **farmer**.   **farm + er = farmer**

1. Which spelling words have these meanings?

a. Person who preaches. ___preacher___

b. Person who drives. ___driver___

2. Use the suffix **-er** to build nouns with these meanings. You will sometimes need to double the final consonant.

a. Person who teaches. ___teacher___

b. Person who helps. ___helper___

c. Person who wins. ___winner___

d. Person who reads. ___reader___

e. Person who plays. ___player___

f. Person who robs. ___robber___

g. Person who works. ___worker___

h. Person who runs. ___runner___

3. In which REVIEW WORD was **e** dropped before **-er** was added? ___driver___

• **Possessive Nouns**
To make a noun show possession, add an apostrophe and **s**.
the book that the teacher owns = the teacher's book
This is a shorter way to show that someone owns something.

4. Write spelling words to finish the phrases below. Remember to use apostrophes.

   a. the garden belonging to my grandma

   my ___grandma's___ garden

   b. the pencil that the teacher has

   the ___teacher's___ pencil

5. Write these phrases a short way by using possessive nouns.

   a. the cellar that belongs to my grandpa

   ___my grandpa's cellar___

   b. the name of the preacher

   ___the preacher's name___

   c. the surprise that the driver had

   ___the driver's surprise___

   d. the enemy of a deer

   ___a deer's enemy___

   e. the color of an earthworm

   ___an earthworm's color___

   f. an arithmetic paper belonging to Kevin

   ___Kevin's arithmetic paper___

Bible Thoughts

Use spelling words to complete these sentences.

6. The three persons of the ___Trinity___ are God the Father, Jesus the Son, and the Holy Spirit.

7. God told Elijah that there were still seven ___thousand___ people in Israel who had not bowed to Baal (1 Kings 19:18).

LESSON 20

NEW WORDS

friends   orange
friend's   caught
farmers   glory
farmer's   smaller
seesaw   enemies
because   forty
chalkboard   naughty
brought   adore

REVIEW WORDS

cloth   lawn
costs   straw

/ˈlônch/

A. Sounds and Letters

- Common spellings of /ô/, as in **saw**, are **a**, **o**, **au**, and **aw**.
  sm<u>a</u>ll **cl<u>o</u>th** **bec<u>au</u>se** **l<u>aw</u>n**
  At the end of a word, /ô/ is usually spelled **aw**.
  s<u>aw</u> **str<u>aw</u>**
  Before the /t/ sound, /ô/ is sometimes spelled **augh** or **ough**.
  c<u>augh</u>t **br<u>ough</u>t**

1. In the following list, print the letter or letters that spell /ô/ in each spelling word. Then write the whole word.

ch_<u>a</u>_lkboard   chalkboard

sm_<u>a</u>_ller   smaller

cl_<u>o</u>_th   cloth

c_<u>o</u>_sts   costs

bec_<u>au</u>_se   because

l_<u>aw</u>_n   lawn

sees_<u>aw</u>_   seesaw

str_<u>aw</u>_   straw

2. Two words that you wrote end with /ô/. Write those words again.

    seesaw   straw

3. Write the spelling words that have /ôt/ spelled **aught**.

    caught   naughty

4. Write the spelling word that has /ôt/ spelled **ought**.

    brought

- The /ôr/ sound, as in **fork**, is usually spelled **or** or **ore**.
  s<u>or</u>t **ad<u>ore</u>**

5. Write the spelling words that have /ôr/ spelled **or**.
    orange
    glory   forty

A. 34 points

80

Test Sentences

1. *glory*   "The *glory* gates are ever open wide."
2. *because*   "We love him, *because* he first loved us."
3. *brought*   Sick people were *brought* to Jesus.
4. *adore*   "O come, let us *adore* Him!"
5. *enemies*   "Love your *enemies*," Jesus said.
6. *forty*   God sent rain for *forty* days.
7. *friends*   Job's *friends* did not speak at first.
8. *friend's*   Her *friend's* house is made of adobe.
9. *farmer's*   A ladybug is a *farmer's* friend.
10. *farmers*   Many *farmers* live in Central America.
11. *caught*   The men *caught* the latex in a cup.
12. *smaller*   A wren is *smaller* than a robin.

6. Which spelling word has /ôr/ spelled **ore** at the end of the word? _____adore_____

7. Write the compound spelling word in which you hear /ôr/. _____chalkboard_____
Which three letters spell /ôr/? ___oar___

8. Which NEW WORDS have /e/ spelled **ie**?
_____friends_____ _____friend's_____

9. Which NEW WORD has three syllables?
_____enemies_____ What is the vowel in the middle syllable? _e_

Write spelling words for these phonetic spellings.

10. ôr′inj _____orange_____

11. smôl′ər _____smaller_____

12. ə dôr′ _____adore_____

B. Using Your Words

B. 23 points

Fill in the blanks with spelling words from the first column.

"A man that hath **(1)** ___friends___ must shew himself friendly" (Proverbs 18:24). Gladys was sad. It seemed that Janet and Kathryn did not want to be her friends. So when Janet and Kathryn played on the **(2)** ___seesaw___, Gladys walked the other way. When Janet and Kathryn drew pictures on the **(3)** ___chalkboard___, Gladys would not help. Gladys's mother saw what was happening and told Gladys to memorize Proverbs 18:24. Soon Gladys realized that Janet and Kathryn seemed unfriendly **(4)** ___because___ she herself was unfriendly. Then Gladys willingly joined the girls in their play. This **(5)** ___brought___ happiness, not only to Gladys but also to Janet and Kathryn. Now all three of them were friends.

6. Write two sentences of your own. Use **cloth** and **chalkboard** in the first sentence. Use **smaller** and **lawn** in the second sentence.

a. _____(Individual sentences.)_____

b. _____

81

13. *orange*   The pack rat took the *orange* button.
14. *seesaw*   A *seesaw* is also called a teeter-totter.
15. *naughty*   We put the *naughty* puppy outside.
16. *chalkboard* Is our *chalkboard* a blackboard?

Why do you put *straw* on the *lawn?*

That *cloth costs* two dollars.

7. Fill in each blank with **four** or **forty**.

  a. The Israelites wandered in the wilderness _____forty_____ years (Numbers 14:33).

  b. A sick man was brought to Jesus by _____four_____ men (Mark 2:3).

  c. Jesus fed _____four_____ thousand people with seven loaves (Matthew 16:10).

  d. Jesus fasted _____forty_____ days and _____forty_____ nights (Matthew 4:2).

8. In each pair, write the spelling word from the first sentence that correctly completes the second sentence.

  a. My juicy orange was very delicious.

   Use _____orange_____ paint for the sunset.

  b. Grandmother is in glory with Jesus.

   "Fear God, and give _____glory_____ to him" (Revelation 14:7).

  c. Shall we use paper or cloth towels?

   Mother got a new _____cloth_____ for the table.

  d. William put clean straw into the pens.

   Ira has a new _____straw_____ hat.

  e. Do not walk on the new lawn.

   Our _____lawn_____ mower is old.

  f. A smile costs nothing and means much.

   The men shared the _____costs_____ of the tools.

9. Complete the sentences with spelling words that are antonyms of the underlined words.

  a. The boy was not <u>obedient</u>; he was _____naughty_____.

  b. We <u>hate</u> evil, but we _____adore_____ Jesus.

  c. I <u>threw</u> the ball, and Charles _____caught_____ it.

C. Building Words

C. 20 points

1. Plural nouns name more than one person, place, or thing. Write the plural forms of the nouns shown here. For some you will add **-s**, for some you will add **-es**, and for some you will change **y** to **i** and add **-es**.

thousand _____thousands_____

dress _____dresses_____

holiday _____holidays_____

supply _____supplies_____

watch _____watches_____

company _____companies_____

- **Plural and Possessive Forms**
  The **-s** that forms plural or possessive nouns has either a /s/ or a /z/ sound.

  many ant<u>s</u>   the ant<u>'s</u> head
  all the boy<u>s</u>   that boy<u>'s</u> arm

  To decide whether you should add **s** or **'s** to a noun, think whether it names more than one or shows possession.

2. Write each boldface word. Use either **s** or **'s** to spell /s/ and /z/.

a. Our **teacher/z/** help us to read the Bible correctly. _____teachers_____

b. Our **teacher/z/** voice is kind and gentle.

_____teacher's_____

Write the correct words in the blanks.

3. friends, friend's

We thank God for _____friends_____.
The path to a _____friend's_____ house is never long.

4. cousins, cousin's

My _____cousin's_____ father is my uncle.
My _____cousins_____ are my uncle's children.

5. farmers, farmer's

A _____farmer's_____ day begins early.
Some _____farmers_____ milk cows.

6. enemies, enemy's

Stephen prayed for his _____enemies_____ before he died.
The porcupine could see his _____enemy's_____ shadow.

7. families, family's

The _____families_____ take turns cleaning the church house.
Our _____family's_____ turn is next week.

Bible Thoughts

Use spelling words to complete these sentences.

8. At Jesus' birth, the shepherds heard the angels say, "_____Glory_____ to God in the highest, and on earth peace, good will toward men" (Luke 2:14).

9. Jesus said, "Love your _____enemies_____, do good to them which hate you" (Luke 6:27).

LESSON 21

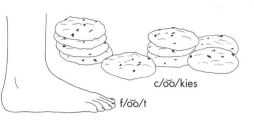

c/o͞o/kies

f/o͝o/t

NEW WORDS

you're	couldn't
wouldn't	haven't
cookies	during
woman	pudding
should	inch in.
fully	foot ft.
pulled	yard yd.
wool	mile mi.

REVIEW WORDS

stood	could
your	wolf

A. Sounds and Letters

- Common spellings of /o͝o/, as in **book**, are **u**, **oo**, **ou**, and **o**.
  fu**ll f**oo**t sh**ou**ld w**o**lf**

1. Write two spelling words that begin with **w** and have /o͝o/ spelled **o**.

   woman   wolf

2. Write the spelling word that begins with **w** and has /o͝o/ spelled **oo**.   wool

3. Write the spelling words that have oo and rhyme with the following words.

   wood _____ stood _____

   put _____ foot _____

4. Write four spelling words that have /o͞o/ spelled **u**.

   fully   during

   pulled   pudding

5. Write six spelling words that have /o͞o/ spelled **ou**.

   you're   couldn't

   wouldn't   your

   should   could

6. Write the two-syllable spelling word containing **oo**.   cookies

7. Write the spelling words that have double consonants.   fully

   pulled   pudding

Write spelling words for these phonetic spellings.

8. sho͝od _____ should _____

9. ko͝od′ənt _____ couldn't _____

10. hav′ənt _____ haven't _____

11. wo͝om′ən _____ woman _____

12. mīl _____ mile _____

13. yärd _____ yard _____

A. 25 points

84

Test Sentences

1.	*cookies*	Mother made *cookies* yesterday.
2.	*should*	Pencil lead *should* be called graphite.
3.	*wool*	A sheep's *wool* is sheared once a year.
4.	*pudding*	We gave our *pudding* to the travelers.
5.	*during*	Woodchucks hibernate *during* the winter.
6.	*fully*	A *fully* grown hummingbird is quite small.
7.	*wouldn't*	Plants *wouldn't* grow without light.
8.	*couldn't*	I *couldn't* read the Braille message.
9.	*you're*	No, *you're* not to eat the leaves.
10.	*haven't*	The word *haven't* is a contraction.
11.	*pulled*	Men *pulled* Jeremiah up from the dungeon.
12.	*woman*	Jesus asked the *woman* for a drink.

B. Using Your Words

B. 29 points

Fill in the blanks with spelling words from the first column.

"Be sure **(1)** __your__ sin will find you out" (Numbers 32:23). Michael rushed

into the house, eager to tell Mother about the new game they had played at school.

Mother was not home, but Michael saw some chocolate chip **(2)** __cookies__ on the

counter. A note was beside the cookies: "Do not touch." Michael **(3)** __stood__

there and eyed the cookies. He was so hungry. Mother **(4)** __wouldn't__ know if he

took only one, he thought.

Slowly Michael ate a warm cookie, but somehow it was not as delicious as he thought

it would be. Just then Mother returned with the mail. One look at Michael's chocolate-

smeared mouth told her that he had eaten a cookie. Mother said sadly, "Michael,

(5) __you're__ old enough to read and obey orders. Because you disobeyed, you

will need to be punished."

6. Write two sentences of your own. Use **woman** and **couldn't** in the first sentence. Use **your** and
pudding in the second sentence.

a. _____ (Individual sentences.) _____

b. _____

7. One spelling word has all these meanings.

(1) The part of a leg on which a person or
animal stands.

(2) The lowest part.

(3) The part opposite the head of something.

(4) Twelve inches.

Write that word in the blank in each sentence. After the sentence, write the number
of the meaning the word has.

a. Arlin needed a __foot__ of wire to
mend the broken fence. __4__

b. Every night I place my shoes at the
__foot__ of my bed. __3__

c. Joseph hurt his __foot__ when he
stepped on a nail. __1__

d. We rested at the __foot__ of the
hill. __2__

85

For numbers 13–16, write the word *and* its abbreviation.

13. *inch*   *in.*   I placed the picture an *inch* from the edge.
14. *foot*   *ft.*   We planted the flowers a *foot* apart.
15. *yard*   *yd.*   A *yard* is a little shorter than a meter.
16. *mile*   *mi.*   The Mount of Olives is about a *mile* long.

Could a *wolf* eat a goose?

Your brother *stood* among the bushes.

8. Fill in each blank with the NEW WORD that fits best.

a. a blanket made of ___wool___

b. ___pulled___ the wagon behind me

c. a Christian man or ___woman___

d. not ___fully___ prepared to go

e. a tasty rice ___pudding___

f. snowed ___during___ the night

g. If it ___should___ rain, go inside.

9. Your and **you're** are homophones. Write the correct word in each blank.

a. Be sure ___your___ work is finished.

b. Try to do ___your___ best.

c. Hurry, or ___you're___ going to be late.

d. When ___you're___ reading aloud, speak clearly and distinctly.

e. Write ___your___ name at the top of the paper.

C. Building Words

C. 33 points

> • **Abbreviations**
> You may use the abbreviations **in., ft., yd.,** and **mi.** when doing math papers and when taking notes. These abbreviations stand for both the singular and the plural words.
> **1 inch = 1 in.   4 inches = 4 in.**

1. To save time and space, we sometimes write abbreviations for some words. What abbreviations may we write for **inch, foot, yard,** and **mile**?

___in.___   ___yd.___

___ft.___   ___mi.___

2. When we write letters and stories, we should write out whole words. What words should we usually write instead of **in., ft., yd.,** and **mi.**?

___inch___   ___yard___

___foot___   ___mile___

3. What punctuation mark follows each abbreviation in this lesson? ___period___

4. The abbreviation ___in.___ stands for **inch** or **inches**. The abbreviation ___ft.___ stands for **foot** or **feet**. The abbreviation ___yd.___ stands for ___yard___ or **yards**. The abbreviation ___mi.___ stands for ___mile___ or **miles**.

5. Write these number sentences, using abbreviations.

12 inches = 1 foot ___12 in. = 1 ft.___

36 inches = 1 yard ___36 in. = 1 yd.___

3 feet = 1 yard ___3 ft. = 1 yd.___

5,280 feet = 1 mile ___5,280 ft. = 1 mi.___

• **Contractions**
To write a contraction, join the two words and use an apostrophe in the place of the letters you leave out.
  is not—isn't   are not—aren't

---

6. Write the spelling word that is a contraction

of **you are**. ___you're___

What letter did you leave out where you put

the apostrophe? ___a___

• Usually when a verb and **not** form a contraction, the **o** is replaced by the apostrophe.
  have not—haven't
  could not—couldn't

---

7. Write contractions for these words. Use an apostrophe to replace the **o** in **not**.

had not ___hadn't___

has not ___hasn't___

should not ___shouldn't___

8. In the word list, find contractions of the underlined words. Answer the questions, using the contractions. The first one is done for you.

a. <u>Could</u> the duck <u>not</u> swim?

The duck couldn't swim.

b. <u>Could</u> the wolf <u>not</u> run?

___The wolf couldn't run.___

c. <u>Would</u> your rope <u>not</u> reach?

___Your rope wouldn't reach.___

d. <u>Have</u> the cookies <u>not</u> been baked?

___The cookies haven't been baked.___

Bible Thoughts

Use spelling words to complete these verses.

9. "And whosoever shall compel thee to go a

___mile___, go with him twain"

(Matthew 5:41).

10. "But he that is an hireling, and not the shepherd, whose own the sheep are not, seeth

the ___wolf___ coming, and leaveth

the sheep, and fleeth" (John 10:12).

5. Allow 2 points per number sentence.

LESSON 22

NEW WORDS

ground
enjoying
joined
crowd
boy's
aren't
wasn't
won't

mouth
counter
cannot
points
hour hr.
week wk.
month mo.
year yr.

REVIEW WORDS

flower
flour

spoil
plow

cl/ou/d   c/ou/   t/oi/

p/oi/nt

_____enjoying_____   _____boy's_____

Now write each word without the suffix.

_____enjoy_____   _____boy_____

> • The /ou/ sound, as in **cow**, is usually spelled **ou** or **ow**.
>   c**ou**nt   cr**ow**d
>   At the end of a word, /ou/ is usually spelled **ow**.
>   c**ow**   h**ow**

A. Sounds and Letters

> • The /oi/ sound, as in **toy**, is spelled **oi** or **oy**. p**oi**nt enj**oy**
> At the beginning of a word or within a word, /oi/ is usually spelled **oi**. **oi**ntment t**oi**l
> At the end of a word, /oi/ is spelled **oy**. t**oy**

1. Write three spelling words that contain the /oi/ sound spelled **oi**. _____joined_____

_____points_____   _____spoil_____

2. Write two spelling words that ended with /oi/ spelled **oy** before a suffix was added.

3. Write five spelling words that contain the /ou/ sound spelled **ou**. _____ground_____

_____mouth_____   _____hour_____

_____counter_____   _____flour_____

4. Write two spelling words that contain the /ou/ sound spelled **ow** within the word.

_____crowd_____   _____flower_____

Now write a REVIEW WORD that ends with the /ou/ sound spelled **ow**. _____plow_____

5. Write the NEW WORDS that rhyme with **near** and with **seek**.

_____year_____   _____week_____

6. Write the NEW WORD that begins with **h** but not the /h/ sound. _____hour_____

A. 28 points

88

Test Sentences

1.	*points*	A compass needle always *points* north.
2.	*counter*	The kitchen *counter* is cracked.
3.	*enjoying*	The boys are *enjoying* the ride.
4.	*mouth*	Open your *mouth* wide when you sing.
5.	*cannot*	We *cannot* do wrong and feel right.
6.	*boy's*	The new *boy's* name is Andrew.
7.	*joined*	We *joined* them in singing.
8.	*wasn't*	Alaska *wasn't* a state until 1959.
9.	*aren't*	Why *aren't* you able to locate Greenland?
10.	*won't*	We *won't* be able to see Mount Mitchell.
11.	*crowd*	In the *crowd* was a woman who needed Jesus.
12.	*ground*	Saul fell to the *ground* and prayed.

7. Which NEW WORDS end with /t/?

___aren't___   ___won't___

___wasn't___   ___cannot___

Write spelling words for these phonetic spellings.

8. munth ___month___

9. yîr ___year___

10. koun'tər ___counter___

11. plou ___plow___

12. kan'ot ___cannot___

13. wēk ___week___

B. Using Your Words

B. 22 points

Fill in the blanks with spelling words from the first column.

"My son, if sinners entice thee, consent thou not" (Proverbs 1:10). Mother wanted to make bread and then discovered that the flour was all gone. So she sent Ray to the store several blocks away to buy some **(1)** ___flour___. Close to the store, Ray saw a **(2)** ___crowd___ of boys. They had cornered a dog and were **(3)** ___enjoying___ their game of throwing sticks and stones at it. A boy who knew Ray said, "Come join us. This is fun."

Ray answered, "I **(4)** ___won't___ join you. Hurting and teasing animals is very cruel." The other **(5)** ___boy's___ unkind answer made Ray feel unhappy, but he went on to the store and bought the flour.

6. Write two sentences of your own. Use **flower** and **ground** in the first sentence. Use **month** and **year** in the second sentence.

a. ___(Individual sentences.)___

b. _____

7. Write spelling words that are synonyms for the boldface words.

a. **earth**   Mother plants seeds in the soft ___ground___.

b. **cultivate**   In spring, the farmers are eager to ___plow___ the soil.

c. **damage**   Stepping on berry plants may ___spoil___ them.

89

For numbers 13–16, write the word *and* its abbreviation.

13. *hour*   hr.   "I need Thee ev'ry *hour,* / Most gracious Lord."
14. *week*   wk.   The first day of the *week,* Jesus arose.
15. *month*   mo.   For *month,* the Indian said "moon."
16. *year*   yr.   For over a *year,* Ezekiel lay on his side.

John will buy *flour* and a *plow.*

Why did you *spoil* that pretty *flower?*

d. **connected**   We saw a long bridge that

___joined___   the island to the mainland.

e. **opening**   Bushes hid the ___mouth___ of the cave.

f. **table**   The clerk rolled out the material on a ___counter___ and measured it.

g. **aims**   The hunter ___points___ the gun at the pheasant and shoots quickly.

8. **Hour—our**, **week—weak**, and **flower—flour** are pairs of homophones. Write the correct word in each blank.

a. We had recess an ___hour___ ago.

b. Whole-wheat ___flour___ makes good bread.

c. On a hike, Joan found a rare ___flower___.

d. The sick man was too ___weak___ to sit up.

e. We try to keep ___our___ books clean.

f. One ___week___ is seven days.

C. Building Words

- **Abbreviations**
  You may use the abbreviations **hr., wk., mo.,** and **yr.** when doing math papers and when taking notes. In letters and stories, it is more proper to write entire words.

1. Write the NEW WORDS that can be abbreviated. Then write their abbreviations.

hour	hr.
week	wk.
month	mo.
year	yr.

2. How should you write **hour** in a letter?

___hour___   How may you write **hour** on a math paper? ___hr.___

- **The abbreviations hr., wk., mo., and yr. stand for both the singular and the plural words.**
  1 year = 1 yr.   3 years = 3 yr.

3. Write these number sentences, using abbreviations for the underlined words. Use **min.** for **minutes**.

60 <u>minutes</u> = 1 <u>hour</u>   ___60 min. = 1 hr.___

24 <u>hours</u> = 1 day   ___24 hr. = 1 day___

7 days = 1 <u>week</u>   ___7 days = 1 wk.___

C. 32 points

3. Allow 2 points for each number sentence containing two abbreviations.

365 days = 1 <u>year</u>   <u>365 days = 1 yr.</u>

4 <u>weeks</u> = 1 <u>month</u>   <u>4 wk. = 1 mo.</u>

52 <u>weeks</u> = 1 <u>year</u>   <u>52 wk. = 1 yr.</u>

12 <u>months</u> = 1 <u>year</u>   <u>12 mo. = 1 yr.</u>

• **Contractions**
When the full word **not** follows a verb, it is always written as a separate word except in the word **cannot**.

was not   are not   cannot

---

4. Which spelling words are contractions of **are not** and **was not**?

<u>aren't</u>   <u>wasn't</u>

What letter did you leave out at the apostrophe when you wrote the contractions? <u>o</u>

5. Write the contraction of **will not**. It does not follow the normal pattern.

<u>won't</u>

6. Write **can't**. <u>can't</u>   **Can't** is a contraction of which NEW WORD?

<u>cannot</u>

Which two letters does the apostrophe replace? <u>no</u>

7. Usually when the full word **not** is used with a verb, the two words are written separately.

has not   is not

Which NEW WORD is an exception to this pattern? <u>cannot</u>

8. Which NEW WORD has an apostrophe but is not a contraction? <u>boy's</u>

Bible Thoughts

Use spelling words to complete these verses.

9. "Let the brother of low degree rejoice in that he is exalted: but the rich, in that he is made low: because as the <u>flower</u> of the grass he shall pass away" (James 1:9, 10).

10. "No man can serve two masters: for either he will hate the one, and love the other; or else he will hold to the one, and despise the other. Ye <u>cannot</u> serve God and mammon" (Matthew 6:24).

LESSON 23

NEW WORDS

enjoyed

vegetables

bridge

changed

I'll

doesn't

didn't

that's

charge

edge

oranges

giant

package

Ave.

St.

Rd.

REVIEW WORDS

huge

strange

jelly

stage

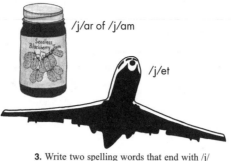

/j/ar of /j/am

/j/et

A. Sounds and Letters

- Common spellings of /j/ are **g**, **j**, **ge**, and **dge**.

    gentle join ca<u>g</u>e bri<u>dge</u>

    At the end of a word, /j/ is usually spelled **dge** after a short vowel sound. **e<u>dge</u> ju<u>dge</u>**

    After a long vowel or a consonant, /j/ is usually spelled **ge**.

    hu<u>ge</u>   chan<u>ge</u>

1. In which two spelling words is /j/ spelled **j**?

    ____enjoyed____   ____jelly____

2. Which NEW WORD begins with /j/ spelled **g**?

    _____giant_____

3. Write two spelling words that end with /j/ spelled **dge**. _____bridge_____

    ____edge____ Does a short or long vowel sound come before **dge**? ___short___

4. Write three REVIEW WORDS that end with /j/ spelled **ge**. _____huge_____

    ____strange____   ____stage____

    Does a short or long vowel sound come before **ge**? ___long___

5. Write two NEW WORDS that end with /j/ spelled **ge**.

    ____charge____   ____package____

6. Which two spelling words ended with **ge** before the suffixes **-ed** and **-s** were added?

    ____changed____   ____oranges____

7. Write the three-syllable spelling word that contains the /j/ sound. ____vegetables____

    What word beginning with **t** do you see at the end of this word? ____table(s)____

8. Which REVIEW WORD has a double consonant? ____jelly____

A. 24 points

92

Test Sentences

1.	*I'll*	The people sang, *"I'll* live for Him."
2.	*didn't*	The woman *didn't* find it difficult.
3.	*doesn't*	Why *doesn't* it stay warm all year?
4.	*that's*	The woman said, "Why, *that's* my coin!"
5.	*giant*	David was not afraid of the *giant* Goliath.
6.	*charge*	Did the publican *charge* too much money?
7.	*bridge*	One *bridge* is twenty-eight miles long.
8.	*enjoyed*	Yesterday we *enjoyed* playing outdoors.
9.	*vegetables*	Some *vegetables* have long roots.
10.	*edge*	The *edge* of the sword is very sharp.
11.	*changed*	A dike *changed* the swamp to farmland.
12.	*oranges*	Eating *oranges* gives you vitamin C.

Write spelling words for these phonetic spellings.

9. pak′ij _____package_____

10. jī′ənt _____giant_____

11. īl _____I'll_____

12. vej′tə bəlz _____vegetables_____

13. brij _____bridge_____

14. thats _____that's_____

15. stāj _____stage_____

B. Using Your Words

B. 25 points

Fill in the blanks with spelling words from the first column.

"In every thing give thanks" (1 Thessalonians 5:18). Wilmer and Lucille could hardly wait until Friday evening. Then the family would visit Uncle Norman's. They (1) __enjoyed__ playing with their cousins. Suddenly Father had an accident that (2) __changed__ their plans. Just after he drove his tractor across a (3) __bridge__ over a small creek, a truck loaded with (4) __vegetables__ hit him. Father was not badly injured, but he had a broken leg. Lucille looked at Wilmer and said, "I am disappointed that we cannot visit Uncle Norman's, but I am thankful that Father (5) __didn't__ get hurt more seriously."

6. Write two sentences of your own. Use **oranges** and **package** in the first sentence. Use **that's** and **strange** in the second sentence.

a. _____(Individual sentences.)_____

b. _____

7. Write the correct spelling word for each clue.

a. Something sweet to spread on bread.

_____jelly_____

b. What we can get juice from.

_____oranges_____

c. What kind of person Goliath was.

_____giant _or_ huge_____

d. How you would feel in a different country. _____strange_____

e. What a whale or an elephant is.

_____huge _or_ giant_____

93

13. *package*   Dennis delivered the *package* to her.

For numbers 14–16, write *only* the abbreviations of the words.

14. *St.*   *(Street)*   Main *Street* crosses Mountain Road.
15. *Ave.*   *(Avenue)*   Go to Third *Avenue* and turn left.
16. *Rd.*   *(Road)*   Spring Valley *Road* runs north and south.

Is it *strange* to make berries into *jelly*?

That *huge stage* is all wood.

f. What a storekeeper will do to get money.

_____ charge _____

g. Something you can wrap or open.

_____ package _____

h. Where a person can stand to give a talk.

_____ stage _____

8. One spelling word has all these meanings.
   (1) The part farthest from the middle.
   (2) A thin side that cuts.
   (3) Move sideways.
   (4) Move little by little.

Write that word in the blank in each sentence. After the sentence, write the number of the meaning the word has.

a. Little Sandra hurt herself with the

_____ edge _____ of the knife. _2_

b. I needed to _____ edge _____ my way

through the narrow opening. _3_

c. We should always leave a margin at the

_____ edge _____ of a paper. _1_

d. I saw the cat _____ edge _____ closer and

closer to the bird. _4_

C. Building Words

C. 26 points

- **Abbreviations**
  The words **Avenue, Street,** and **Road** may be abbreviated as **Ave., St.,** and **Rd.** on charts and other such places where there is not room to write entire words. In letters and stories, the words should be spelled out.

1. Write the abbreviation from the spelling list for each word.

Avenue _____ Ave. _____

Street _St._   **Road** _Rd._

2. The following words start with capital letters. Write these proper nouns, but abbreviate each underlined word.

Main <u>Street</u> _____ Main St. _____

Oak <u>Avenue</u> _____ Oak Ave. _____

Forest <u>Road</u> _____ Forest Rd. _____

Shell <u>Avenue</u> _____ Shell Ave. _____

Railroad <u>Street</u> _____ Railroad St. _____

Spring <u>Road</u> _____ Spring Rd. _____

• The words **avenue, street,** and **road** should not be abbreviated when they are common nouns. This is a narrow **street**.

3. Write the correct word for each sentence.

a. Stop, look, and listen before you cross the (street, St.). ____street____

b. This is a busy (Rd., road). ___road___

• **Contractions**
When a pronoun and **will** or **shall** form a contraction, the apostrophe replaces **wi** or **sha**.
   I will—I'll   he will—he'll
   I shall—I'll

4. Which NEW WORD is a contraction of **I will** or **I shall**? ___I'll___

When **I will** is written as **I'll**, what letters does the apostrophe replace? ___wi___

When **I shall** is written as **I'll**, what letters does the apostrophe replace? ___sha___

5. Write the contractions of these words.

you will _____you'll_____

he will _____he'll_____

she will _____she'll_____

it will _____it'll_____

we will _____we'll_____

they will _____they'll_____

who will _____who'll_____

6. Write the NEW WORDS that are contractions of these words.

did not _____didn't_____

does not _____doesn't_____

that is _____that's_____

Bible Thoughts

Use spelling words to complete these verses.

7. "How shall we sing the LORD's song in a ___strange___ land?" (Psalm 137:4).

8. "For he shall give his angels __charge__ over thee, to keep thee in all thy ways" (Psalm 91:11).

LESSON 24

19	20	21	22	23
Mennonite	friends	you're	ground	enjoyed
arithmetic	friend's	wouldn't	enjoying	vegetables
supply	farmers	cookies	joined	bridge
among	farmer's	woman	crowd	changed
preacher	seesaw	should	boy's	I'll
teacher's	because	fully	aren't	doesn't
grandma's	chalkboard	pulled	wasn't	didn't
surprise	brought	wool	won't	that's
Trinity	orange	couldn't	mouth	charge
balloon	caught	haven't	counter	edge
company	glory	during	cannot	oranges
enemy	smaller	pudding	points	giant
holiday	enemies	inch in.	hour hr.	package
interesting	forty	foot ft.	week wk.	Ave.
sugar	naughty	yard yd.	month mo.	St.
different	adore	mile mi.	year yr.	Rd.

A. Sounds and Letters Review

A. 38 points

1. Complete these sentences with words from Lesson 19 that have /ə/ in them.

   a. To the teacher's ___surprise___, Joan finished her ___arithmetic___ lesson early.

   b. A green ___balloon___ was ___among___ Glenn's treasures.

   c. Our ___supply___ of ___sugar___ was too small to make a cake.

   d. We enjoy having ___company___ at our house even when it is not Thanksgiving or a ___different___ holiday.

2. Complete these sentences with words from Lesson 20 that have /ô/ in them.

   a. The ___chalkboard___ needed washing ___because___ it was so dusty.

   b. John ___caught___ a lizard and ___brought___ it to school in a jar.

   c. How can a ___smaller___ boy and a larger boy balance on a ___seesaw___?

3. Complete these sentences with words from Lesson 21 that have /o͞o/ in them.

   a. The kind ___woman___ gave a dozen ___cookies___ to the children.

96

Review—Test Sentences

1. *week* — The carpenter worked a *week* on the roof.
2. *year* — Next *year* will come soon enough.
3. *foot* — That is the wrong *foot* for this shoe.
4. *cannot* — Without a key, you *cannot* unlock it.
5. *hour* — We don't know what *hour* Jesus will come.
6. *pulled* — The tractor *pulled* the wagon.
7. *won't* — My pen *won't* write any more.
8. *ground* — The multitude sat on the *ground* to eat.
9. *brought* — Wise men *brought* gifts to Jesus.
10. *because* — They worshiped Him *because* He is King.
11. *farmers* — Two *farmers* are plowing.
12. *didn't* — People *didn't* always have automobiles.

b. A good farmer ___wouldn't___ shear

his sheep's ___wool___ in winter.

c. This soft ___pudding___ will be firm

after it has ___fully___ set.

4. Complete these sentences with words from Lesson 22 that have /ou/ in them.

a. A ___crowd___ of people gathered

at the front ___counter___ in the store.

b. Part of my ___mouth___ was numb

for over an ___hour___ after my

visit to the dentist.

5. Complete these sentences with words from Lesson 22 that have /oi/ in them.

a. The sharp ___points___ on the

barbed wire tore holes in the ___boy's___

shirt.

b. The children were ___enjoying___

their game even before their cousins

___joined___ them.

6. Complete these sentences with words from Lesson 23 that have /j/ in them.

a. The family ___enjoyed___ fresh

___vegetables___ from the garden.

b. The ___charge___ for crossing the

big ___bridge___ is over two dollars.

c. My uncle brought a ___package___

of delicious ___oranges___ from a

grove in Florida.

Write spelling words for these phonetic spellings.

7. kroud ___crowd___

8. glôr′ē ___glory___

9. ə dôr′ ___adore___

10. chānjd ___changed___

97

13. *chalkboard* Write on the *chalkboard* neatly.
14. *sugar* Pass the *sugar*, please.
15. *joined* The visitors *joined* us in singing.
16. *surprise* Did Grandpa *surprise* you?
17. *enjoying* The children are *enjoying* the story.
18. *package* Hold the *package* carefully.
19. *adore* Praise and *adore* the Lord.
20. *giant* The *giant* Goliath was nearly nine feet tall.
21. *caught* His kite is *caught* in a tree.
22. *crowd* The *crowd* followed Jesus.
23. *wouldn't* The cow *wouldn't* leave her calf.
24. *wool* Sheep need their *wool* in winter.
25. *seesaw* All recess the *seesaw* went up and down.
26. *among* Divide the crackers *among* the children.

B. Using Your Words Review

B. 30 points

Fill in the crossword puzzle with NEW WORDS from Lessons 19–23. You may need to change a singular spelling word to plural or a plural word to singular.

Across

5. Soft, curly hair of sheep. wool
7. Subject dealing with numbers. arithmetic
10. Abbreviation for **Avenue**. Ave.
11. Air-filled rubber toy. balloon
12. Part farthest from the middle. edge
14. Not friends. enemies
17. Sixty minutes. hour
18. Sweet substance made from cane. sugar
20. Soft, cooked food. pudding
22. Father, Son, and Holy Spirit. Trinity
23. Abbreviation for **inch**. in.
24. Twelve months. year
25. Abbreviation for **foot**. ft.
27. Took pleasure in. enjoyed
28. Not a friend. enemy

Down

1. Soil. ground
2. Abbreviation for **Street**. St.
3. For the reason that; since. because
4. Abbreviation for **mile**. mi.
6. A round, juicy fruit. orange
8. Abbreviation for **hour**. hr.
9. Small, flat, sweet cakes. cookies
13. Three feet. yard
15. Member of a certain church. Mennonite
16. Furnish; provide. supply
17. Special day of celebration. holiday
19. Love and admire greatly. adore
20. Bundle of things wrapped together. package
21. Long table in a store. counter
26. Abbreviation for **month**. mo.

Periods after abbreviations are optional on the crossword puzzle.

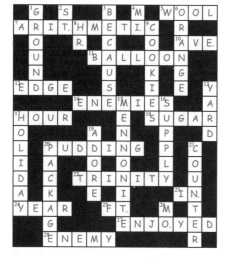

98

27. *arithmetic*   I checked my *arithmetic* paper.
28. *woman*   A *woman* touched the hem of Jesus' garment.
29. *during*   School is closed *during* the summer.
30. *oranges*   We peeled *oranges* for breakfast.
31. *points*   The compass needle *points* north.
32. *charge*   How much did he *charge* for the bread?
33. *changed*   He must have *changed* his mind.
34. *counter*   The clerk behind the *counter* smiled.
35. *that's*   Yes, *that's* the reason.
36. *holiday*   We have no *holiday* today.
37. *supply*   Forests *supply* the country with wood.
38. *bridge*   Flood waters washed the *bridge* away.
39. *teacher's*   Books are on the *teacher's* desk.
40. *balloon*   My sister's *balloon* burst.

C. Building Words Review

1. Join two words from this sentence to form a compound word found in Lesson 20. Use yellow chalk to write your answer on the board. _____chalkboard_____

2. Write each phrase a short way by using a possessive noun.

a. a balloon our friend owns

_____our friend's balloon_____

b. the vegetables of the farmer

_____the farmer's vegetables_____

c. the oranges my grandma has

_____my grandma's oranges_____

3. Decide whether the boldface word is plural or shows possession. Write it correctly.

a. Jesus fed the multitude with the **boy/z/** lunch. _____boy's_____

b. Job's **friend/z/** came to comfort him. _____friends_____

c. The spies said they saw **giant/s/** in Canaan. _____giants_____

d. Our **teacher/z/** name is the same as Jacob's mother's name. __teacher's__

4. Write these proper nouns and number sentences. Abbreviate the underlined words.

Orange <u>Street</u>	Orange St.
Church <u>Road</u>	Church Rd.
Flower <u>Avenue</u>	Flower Ave.

36 <u>inches</u> = 1 <u>yard</u>	36 in. = 1 yd.
5,280 <u>feet</u> = 1 <u>mile</u>	5,280 ft. = 1 mi.
24 <u>hours</u> = 1 day	24 hr. = 1 day
52 <u>weeks</u> = 1 <u>year</u>	52 wk. =1 yr.
12 <u>months</u> = 1 <u>year</u>	12 mo. = 1 yr.

5. Write contractions for these words.

I will	I'll	could not	couldn't
you are	you're	have not	haven't
cannot	can't	was not	wasn't
we shall	we'll	that is	that's

6. Begin each sentence with the contraction of the boldface word and **not**. Remember to use capital letters.

are	Aren't	the boys running?
did	Didn't	the water run?
does	Doesn't	the motor run?
will	Won't	the train run today?

Bible Thoughts

Use spelling words to complete these sentences.

7. Noah was a _____preacher_____ of righteousness (2 Peter 2:5).

8. "When a man's ways please the LORD, he maketh even his _____enemies_____ to be at peace with him" (Proverbs 16:7).

9. Samson _____caught_____ three hundred foxes (Judges 15:4).

99

C. 35 points

4. Allow 2 points for each number sentence containing two abbreviations.

41. *friend's*	We just passed my *friend's* house.
42. *enemy*	The fox is an *enemy* of the rabbit.
43. *enemies*	"Love your *enemies*," Jesus said..
44. *Mennonite*	The sign says *Mennonite* Church.

For numbers 45–50, write *only* the abbreviations of the words.

45. *St.*	*(Street)*	Main *Street*

For numbers 45–50, write only the abbreviations.

46. *Rd.*	*(Road)*	Blue Mountain *Road*
47. *yr.*	*(year)*	twelve months in a *year*

Remember, we are writing abbreviations.

48. *wk.*	*(week)*	seven days in a *week*
49. *mi.*	*(mile)*	five thousand, two hundred eighty feet in a *mile*
50. *ft.*	*(foot)*	twelve inches in a *foot*

LESSON 25

NEW WORDS

grown   recess
since   answer
space   blessing
mercy   lace
chase   blew
absent   crossed
I'd   nurse
he'd   cents

REVIEW WORDS

basket   grew
twice   rang

A. Sounds and Letters

/s/aw   /s/un

> • Common spellings of /s/ are **s**, **c**,
> **se**, **ce**, and **ss**.   <u>s</u>aw   <u>c</u>ent
>   nur<u>se</u>   twi<u>ce</u>   cro<u>ss</u>
> At the end of a word, /s/ is
> usually spelled **ss** after a short
> vowel sound, but **se** or **ce** after
> any other sound.
>   ble<u>ss</u>   mi<u>ss</u>   cha<u>se</u>   spi<u>ce</u>

1. Write three spelling words that begin with
/s/ spelled **s** or **c**. ____since____

____space____   ____cents____

2. Write four spelling words that have a final
/s/ spelled **ce**.

____since____   ____lace____

____space____   ____twice____

3. Write two spelling words that have a final
/s/ spelled **se**.

____chase____   ____nurse____

4. Write the NEW WORDS that have /s/ spelled
ss.   ____recess____

____blessing____   ____crossed____

5. Write the two-syllable spelling words that
have /s/ spelled **c**.

____mercy____   ____recess____

6. Write the two-syllable spelling words that
have /s/ spelled **s**.

____absent____   ____basket____

7. Write the two-syllable spelling word that
has /s/ spelled **sw**.   ____answer____

8. Which spelling words contain **nt**?

____absent____   ____cents____

9. Which spelling word

a. ends with **et**? ____basket____

b. begins with **ab**? ____absent____

A. 26 points

Test Sentences

1.	*blessing*	We ask a *blessing* on our food.
2.	*crossed*	Jesus *crossed* the brook to pray.
3.	*mercy*	The lepers said, "Have *mercy* on us."
4.	*he'd*	The prodigal son decided *he'd* go back home.
5.	*chase*	The dog might *chase* the rabbit.
6.	*absent*	Is anyone *absent* today?
7.	*I'd*	I believe *I'd* choose green.
8.	*space*	The first *space* is called F.
9.	*recess*	During *recess* we play tag.
10.	*answer*	Jesus gave the men a good *answer*.
11.	*grown*	Many potatoes are *grown* in Idaho.
12.	*lace*	Flowers are prettier than *lace* and ribbons.

Write spelling words for these phonetic spellings.

10. hēd _____ he'd _____

11. blo͞o _____ blew _____

12. īd _____ I'd _____

13. rang _____ rang _____

14. grōn _____ grown _____

B. Using Your Words

B. 19 points

Fill in the blanks with spelling words from the first column.

The ostrich is the largest living bird. Some ostriches have **(1)** _grown_ to be nearly eight feet tall. The ostrich is called the camel bird, **(2)** _since_ it can go a long time without water. When people **(3)** _chase_ an ostrich to try to capture it, the ostrich does something that seems foolish. It runs in a circle, which makes it easier to catch. An ostrich egg is very large. It is much more than **(4)** _twice_ as large as a chicken egg. The father ostrich digs a hole in the sand for the eggs. Then several hens lay eggs in the same nest. During the day, when the father is **(5)** _absent_, the mothers take turns keeping the eggs warm. God surely made the ostrich an interesting bird.

6. Write two sentences of your own. Use **rang** and **recess** in the first sentence. Use **space** and **basket** in the second sentence.

a. _____ (Individual sentences.) _____

b. _____

7. Use the homophones **grown** and **groan** in the following sentences.

a. The corn had _grown_ six inches in one week.

b. The pain from his broken leg made George _groan_.

c. Cheryl has _grown_ two inches this year.

8. Write NEW WORDS that are homophones for these words.

blue _blew_   heed _he'd_

101

13. *blew*   An east wind *blew* locusts into Egypt.
14. *since*   Arizona is desert, *since* it is hot and dry.
15. *cents*   One hundred *cents* make a dollar.
16. *nurse*   The doctor told the *nurse* what to write.

The bell *rang twice*.

Blue flowers *grew* in the hanging *basket*.

9. Complete each sentence with a spelling word.

a. Timothy willingly put his fifty ___cents___ into the church offering.

b. Mephibosheth was crippled after his ___nurse___ dropped him (2 Samuel 4:4).

c. Try to ___space___ your letters evenly when you write.

d. Being able to attend a Christian school is a ___blessing___.

e. We should play fairly during ___recess___.

C. Building Words

grow grew grown I had I would

C. 35 points

- **Verb Forms**
  The past form of some verbs is made by changing the vowel instead of adding **-ed**.
      see—saw   catch—caught

1. Complete these sentences by adding **-ed** to **bless**, **cross**, **answer**, **chase**, and **lace**.

a. God has ___blessed___ us with sound minds.

b. I have ___crossed___ my *t*'s and *x*'s.

c. Have you ___answered___ all the questions?

d. The butterflies ___chased___ each other in the sunshine.

e. Is your shoe ___laced___?

2. Complete the second sentence in each pair with a spelling word that is a form of the underlined verb in the first sentence.

a. Where did the wind <u>blow</u> the locusts? The wind ___blew___ them into the Red Sea.

b. We knew the bell would soon <u>ring</u>. When it ___rang___, we ran inside.

c. Peas <u>grow</u> well in cool, damp weather. Our peas ___grew___ fast after the rain.

d. Many pine trees <u>grow</u> tall. This tree has not ___grown___ very tall.

3. Use the boldface verbs to complete the sentences correctly.
do, did, done   throw, threw, thrown

a. Nathan can ___throw___ the ball. He ___threw___ it high. He has ___thrown___ it often.

b. David should _____do_____ his chores.

Allen _____did_____ his chores early.

Have you _____done_____ yours?

• **Contractions**

To form a contraction with a pronoun and **had** or **would**, shorten **had** or **would** to **'d**.

I had—I'd   I would—I'd

---

4. Which NEW WORD is a contraction of **I had** or **I would**? _____I'd_____ When **I had** is written as **I'd**, what letters does the apostrophe replace? ___ha___ When **I would** is written as **I'd**, what letters does the apostrophe replace? ___woul___

5. Which NEW WORD is a contraction of **he had** or **he would**? _____he'd_____

6. Write the contractions of these **had** phrases.

I had _____I'd_____

you had _____you'd_____

he had _____he'd_____

she had _____she'd_____

it had _____it'd_____

we had _____we'd_____

they had _____they'd_____

7. Write the contractions of these **would** phrases.

I would _____I'd_____

you would _____you'd_____

he would _____he'd_____

she would _____she'd_____

it would _____it'd_____

we would _____we'd_____

they would _____they'd_____

Bible Thoughts

Use spelling words to complete these sentences.

8. The disciples helped the apostle Paul to escape by letting him down by the wall in a _____basket_____ (Acts 9:25).

9. "But the _____mercy_____ of the LORD is from everlasting to everlasting upon them that fear him" (Psalm 103:17).

LESSON 26

NEW WORDS

noise	wisdom
desert	children
teeth	hose
women	praise
dozen	easy
slept	presents
mouse	reasons
led	taught

REVIEW WORDS

size	zone
mice	bought

 /z/ebra

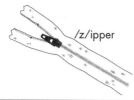 /z/ipper

- At the end of a word, /z/ is usually spelled **zz** after a short vowel sound, but **ze** or **se** after any other sound.

  fuzz   prize   noise

A. Sounds and Letters

- Common spellings of the /z/ sound are **z**, **s**, **ze**, **se**, and **zz**.

  zebra   wisdom   size
  hose   fuzzy

1. In which spelling words is /z/ spelled **z** in the middle or beginning of the word?

_____dozen_____ _____zone_____

2. In which two-syllable spelling words is /z/ spelled **s**?

_____desert_____ _____presents_____

_____wisdom_____ _____reasons_____

_____easy_____

3. How is final /z/ spelled in **buzz**? ___zz___

Is the vowel sound before /z/ **long** or **short**?

_____short_____

4. In which spelling words does final /z/ have these spellings?

se___noise___   _____praise_____

_____hose_____ **ze**___size___

5. Two NEW WORDS end with the plural suffix **-s**. In which word does the suffix have

a. the /z/ sound? _____reasons_____

b. the /s/ sound?_____presents_____

6. Which spelling word means "more than one woman"? _____women_____ In both **woman** and **women**, the first vowel is **o**. That vowel spells /o͞o/ in (woman, women), and it spells /i/ in (woman, women).

7. Write two one-syllable spelling words that have /e/ in them.

_____slept_____ _____led_____

A. 25 points

Test Sentences

1.	*praise*	Psalm 8 is a psalm of *praise* to God.
2.	*children*	"Hosanna!" the *children* sang.
3.	*led*	Moses *led* the Israelites out of Egypt.
4.	*presents*	Wise men brought *presents* to Jesus.
5.	*women*	The Bible says that *women* should not preach.
6.	*wisdom*	How much better is *wisdom* than gold!
7.	*noise*	"Make a joyful *noise* unto the LORD."
8.	*easy*	Was that word *easy* to spell?
9.	*taught*	Jesus *taught* as one having authority.
10.	*slept*	The bear *slept* all winter.
11.	*hose*	With a kink in the *hose,* water cannot flow.
12.	*mouse*	Joy put butter on the trap to catch the *mouse.*

Write spelling words for these phonetic spellings.

10. bôt _____ bought _____

11. tôt _____ taught _____

8. tēth _____ teeth _____

12. noiz _____ noise _____

9. mīs _____ mice _____

B. Using Your Words

B. 28 points

Fill in the blanks with spelling words from the first column.

A small, soft, furry creature that most people dislike is the **(1)** ___ mouse ___ . The word **mouse** comes from a word that means "thief." This sneaky creature makes very little **(2)** ___ noise ___ as it darts around. Mice may be small in **(3)** ___ size ___ , but they can destroy large amounts of food. With their strong, sharp **(4)** ___ teeth ___ they can gnaw their way into many places. Their whiskers help them to feel their way in the dark. In Bible times, **(5)** ___ mice ___ were considered unclean animals and were not to be eaten. Even though many people dislike mice, scientists find them useful in testing new drugs for diseases.

6. Write two sentences of your own. Use **bought** and **dozen** in the first sentence. Use **taught** and **children** in the second sentence.

a. _____ (Individual sentences.) _____

b. _____

7. Write spelling words that fit these clues.

a. The number of eggs in a carton.

___ dozen ___

b. What water goes through.

___ hose ___

c. Where a cactus grows.

___ desert ___

d. What you use to chew.

___ teeth ___

e. What you did last night.

___ slept ___

f. What Solomon requested from God.

___ wisdom ___

g. What you give God when you sing.

___ praise ___

105

13. *teeth*   Your four front *teeth* are called incisors.

14. *dozen*   One and one-half *dozen* is eighteen.

15. *reasons*   There are two *reasons* he cannot come.

16. *desert*   Northern Africa is mostly *desert* land.

A boy *bought* two *mice* for his kittens.

This red line shows the *size* of the *zone*.

8. Match the antonyms by placing the letters in the second column before the correct words in the first column.

_b_	noise	a. ignorance
_d_	women	b. silence
_a_	wisdom	c. sold
_f_	easy	d. men
_c_	bought	e. adults
_e_	children	f. hard

9. Use the words in the first column of exercise 8 to complete these sentences.

a. Some ___women___ carry their babies on their backs.

b. After reading the instructions, Beth found the lesson ___easy___ to do.

c. During the earthquake, there was a frightening ___noise___ .

d. "Be ye therefore followers of God, as dear ___children___ " (Ephesians 5:1).

e. Happiness cannot be ___bought___ with money.

f. "How much better is it to get ___wisdom___ than gold!" (Proverbs 16:16).

C. Building Words

keep | kept | kept | mouse | mice

C. 30 points

Verb Forms

1. Complete the second sentence in each pair by writing the spelling word that is a form of the underlined verb in the first sentence.

a. At night we <u>sleep</u>.

The baby ___slept___ all night.

b. "<u>Teach</u> me thy way, O LORD."

Jesus ___taught___ the disciples.

c. We <u>buy</u> flour by the pound.

Marie ___bought___ ten pounds.

d. These paths both <u>lead</u> to the creek.

Kay ___led___ us to her house.

2. Use the boldface verbs to complete the sentences correctly.

buy   bought   bought
catch   caught   caught

a. I will ___catch___ the ball if I can.

The last time, Jesse ___caught___ it.

He has ___caught___ it several times this afternoon.

b. Father will ___buy___ some fruit at the market. He ___bought___ some pears yesterday. He had ___bought___ some plums last week.

Plural Nouns

3. Complete the sentences with the plural forms of the boldface words.

  a. **present** The Queen of Sheba gave ____presents____ to Solomon.

  b. **reason** Give two ____reasons____ for your answer.

  c. **zone** A large city has several postal ____zones____ .

  d. **praise** Let us sing ____praises____ to God.

4. Some words are not made plural by adding **-s** or **-es**. Write **woman**, **tooth**, **child**, and **mouse**. Beside each word, write the spelling word that is its plural form.

woman	women
tooth	teeth
child	children
mouse	mice

Dictionary Practice

5. Some words are spelled alike but have different meanings. Look at this sentence:

"I walked a **yard** into the **yard**." Two different words are spelled **yard**. Such words have separate entries in a dictionary, numbered like this: **yard**[1] and **yard**[2].

The underlined words in the sentences below have more than one entry in the Speller Dictionary. Write the number of the entry that matches the word in each sentence.

  _2_ a. <u>Pitch</u> the ball to me.

  _2_ b. A <u>fly</u> crawled on the ceiling.

  _2_ c. Please <u>close</u> the window.

  _1_ d. These shoes do not <u>match</u>.

  _3_ e. Things went <u>counter</u> to our plan.

  _2_ f. Soon the bell will <u>ring</u>.

Bible Thoughts

Use spelling words to complete these sentences.

6. Jesus sat in a ship and ____taught____ the people (Luke 5:3).

7. Jesus said, "Suffer the little ____children____ to come unto me, and forbid them not: for of such is the kingdom of God" (Mark 10:14).

LESSON 27

NEW WORDS

forgave
carrying
break
forgotten
choose
pocketbook
trunk
stockings

broke
skates
Christmas
pictures
music
chickens
it's
we're

REVIEW WORDS

shake
picnic

kitchen
crack

/k/ey

/k/a/k/e

du/k/

2. Which NEW WORD begins with /k/ spelled
ch? _____ Christmas _____

3. Write four spellings words that have /k/
spelled **ck**.

_____ pocketbook _____ _____ chickens _____

_____ stockings _____ _____ crack _____

• When /k/ follows a short vowel
and comes at the end of an unaccented syllable, /k/ is usually
spelled **c**. musi**c** publi**c**

4. Write **pictures** and **music**.

_____ pictures _____ _____ music _____

Which of these two words does not totally
follow the rules in this lesson?

_____ pictures _____

5. Which REVIEW WORD has two /k/ sounds
spelled **c**? _____ picnic _____

• When /k/ at the end of a word or
syllable is not preceded by a
short vowel, /k/ is usually spelled
k. trun**k** mee**k** sha**k**e boo**k**

6. Write the compound spelling word that has
/k/ spelled **k** after the /o͞o/ sound.

_____ pocketbook _____

A. Sounds and Letters

• Common spellings of the /k/
sound are **k**, **c**, and **ck**.
mee**k** musi**c** **crack**
When /k/ follows a short vowel
and comes at the end of an
accented syllable or a one-
syllable word, /k/ is usually
spelled **ck**. chi**ck**en **crack**

1. Write three spelling words that begin with
/k/ spelled **k** or **c**. _____ carrying _____

_____ kitchen _____ _____ crack _____

A. 26 points

108

Test Sentences

1. *we're* Now *we're* ready to begin.
2. *pictures* The Bible gives many *pictures* of heaven.
3. *carrying* The dog is *carrying* your shoe away.
4. *pocketbook* The lady's *pocketbook* is lost.
5. *it's* Yes, *it's* your turn.
6. *chickens* Male *chickens* are called roosters.
7. *trunk* Sap flows through the *trunk* of a tree.
8. *stockings* Two *stockings* make a pair.
9. *music* The chirping of birds is *music* to my ear.
10. *skates* A Dutch boy *skates* on the frozen canal.
11. *Christmas* In Peru, *Christmas* is in summer.
12. *forgave* Jesus *forgave* the people who hurt Him.

7. Write three one-syllable spelling words that have /k/ spelled **k** after a long vowel.

_____break_____   _____shake_____

_____broke_____

8. Write the NEW WORD that has /k/ spelled **k** after a consonant. _____trunk_____

9. Which spelling words begin with **for**?

_____forgave_____   _____forgotten_____

Write spelling words for these phonetic spellings.

10. chōōz _____choose_____

11. kich'ən _____kitchen_____

12. wîr _____we're_____

13. skāts _____skates_____

14. myōō'zik _____music_____

15. its _____it's_____

16. brōk _____broke_____

B. Using Your Words

B. 31 points

Fill in the blanks with spelling words from the first column.

An elephant's long, boneless **(1)** ___trunk___ is very useful. With it he can pick up a tiny peanut or untie a knot in a rope. He uses his trunk when **(2)** ___carrying___ heavy loads. After an elephant fills his trunk with water, he may **(3)** ___choose___ to squirt it into his mouth or at something. Elephants have good memories. One elephant had not **(4)** ___forgotten___ how unkindly a certain man had treated him, and later he harmed that man. One way to capture these animals is to dig a pit and cover it with branches and dirt. When the elephant steps on this, he will **(5)** ___break___ through.

6. Write two sentences of your own. Use **broke** and **skates** in the first sentence. Use **trunk** and **stockings** in the second sentence.

a. _____(Individual sentences.)_____

b. _____

7. Write the contraction for **it is**. ___it's___
The apostrophe replaces what letter? _i_

8. The homophone for **it's** is **its**, which means "belonging to it." Write the correct homophone in each sentence.

a. The moth has left ___its___ cocoon.

109

13. *break* In heaven, thieves do not *break* through.
14. *forgotten* Joseph had not *forgotten* Jacob.
15. *choose* David went to *choose* five stones.
16. *broke* Gideon's men *broke* their pitchers.

The walls *crack* when the houses *shake*.

After we clean the *kitchen,* we will go on a *picnic.*

(Teacher: You need not require the comma.)

b. The robin was busily feeding __its__ young.

c. When __it's__ very warm, we sometimes wade in the creek.

9. Fill in the blanks with spelling words.

a. **Gas** is to **tank** as **money** is to __pocketbook__.

b. **Hands** are to **gloves** as **feet** are to __stockings or skates__.

c. **Tomb** is to **Good Friday** as **manger** is to __Christmas__.

d. **Writer** is to **stories** as **artist** is to __pictures__.

e. **Unpleasant** is to **screech** as **pleasant** is to __music__.

f. **Rams** are to **sheep** as **roosters** are to __chickens__.

g. **Winter** is to **skate** as **summer** is to __picnic__.

h. **Wash** is to **laundry room** as **cook** is to __kitchen__.

10. Write the spelling words that mean the opposite of these words and phrases.

a. remembered __forgotten__

b. mended __broke__

c. hold still __shake__

d. held a grudge __forgave__

11. Write these spelling words in alphabetical order.

crack __carrying__

choose __chickens__

Christmas __choose__

carrying __Christmas__

chickens __crack__

C. Building Words

C. 21 points

Verb Forms

1. Complete the second sentence in each pair by writing the spelling word that is a form of the underlined verb in the first sentence.

a. Do not <u>forget</u> to write.

Have you __forgotten__ your lunch?

b. People who love God <u>forgive</u> others.

Jesus __forgave__ the people who crucified Him.

c. Elizabeth is learning to <u>skate</u>.

No one in our family __skates__.

d. Father <u>cracked</u> the coconut.

Jason had tried hard, but he could not

<u>crack</u> it.

e. Can you <u>carry</u> this package for me?

I am <u>carrying</u> too many other

things.

2. Use the boldface verbs to complete the sentences correctly.

break	broke	broken
choose	chose	chosen
shake	shook	shaken

a. Let the others <u>choose</u> first.

God <u>chose</u> David to be king.

Christians have <u>chosen</u> to

serve the Lord.

b. We will <u>shake</u> the rugs. We

<u>shook</u> them yesterday. We

have <u>shaken</u> them often.

c. Please <u>break</u> this in half.

Who <u>broke</u> the plate? Two

boards in the fence are <u>broken</u>.

Contractions and Syllable Divisions

3. Write the NEW WORDS that are contractions for **it is** and **we are**.

<u>it's</u> <u>we're</u>

4. Write the NEW WORDS that have three syllables. Use slashes to divide them into syllables.

<u>car/ry/ing</u> <u>pock/et/book</u>

<u>for/got/ten</u>

Bible Thoughts

Use spelling words to complete these sentences.

5. We must <u>choose</u> to love one

another.

6. Jesus told about a king who <u>forgave</u>

his servant's great debt (Matthew 18:23–27).

Lesson 28—79 points

LESSON 28

/w/asp

/kw/ilt

bo/ks/

NEW WORDS

square
mixed
quickly
language
question
sixteen
unlike
unpainted

wax
cracks
weather
broken
checks
Thanksgiving
disorderly
discolored

REVIEW WORDS

kept
wondered

watched
tracks

A. Sounds and Letters

• The /w/ sound is usually spelled **w**. **wax** **weather**

1. Which spelling words begin with /w/?

_____wax_____ _____wondered_____

_____weather_____ _____watched_____

2. The missing sound in each word is /w/ spelled **w**. Write the words correctly.

a_ake _awake_ re_ard _reward_

be_are _beware_ t_ins _twins_

3. In which spelling word is /w/ spelled **u** after the letter **g**? _____language_____

• The consonant blend /kw/ is usually spelled **qu**.
quick **square**

4. In which NEW WORDS is /kw/ spelled **qu**?

_____square_____ _____question_____

_____quickly_____

• The consonant blend /ks/ is usually spelled **x**. **box** **wax** Adding the suffix **-s** to a root word ending with **k** gives the word the /ks/ sound.
pack—packs **mark—marks**

5. Write the spelling words that have /ks/ spelled **x**. _____mixed_____

_____sixteen_____ _____wax_____

6. Write the NEW WORDS that end with /ks/ because the suffix **-s** was added to root words ending with /k/.

_____cracks_____ _____checks_____

Now write the root words.

_____crack_____ _____check_____

7. Which NEW WORD is a compound in which the first part ends with **k** and the suffix **-s**?

_____Thanksgiving_____

A. 26 points

112

Test Sentences

1.	*checks*	See the pretty *checks* in the tablecloth.
2.	*cracks*	A cold jar *cracks* in hot water.
3.	*square*	A *square* has four equal sides.
4.	*unlike*	It is *unlike* Alvin to be late.
5.	*wax*	When should we *wax* the floor?
6.	*disorderly*	Clean up your *disorderly* desk.
7.	*language*	In the French *language,* "et" means "and."
8.	*Thanksgiving*	*Thanksgiving* Day is in the fall.
9.	*discolored*	Sunlight *discolored* the paper.
10.	*unpainted*	They bought *unpainted* furniture.
11.	*mixed*	Red and yellow *mixed* make orange.
12.	*weather*	God controls the *weather* every day.

8. Write the three-syllable spelling word in which /k/ is spelled **c**. _discolored_

Write spelling words for these phonetic spellings.

9. brō′kən _broken_

10. wocht _watched_

11. kwik′lē _quickly_

12. weth′ər _weather_

13. dis ôr′dər lē _disorderly_

B. 22 points

B. Using Your Words

Fill in the blanks with spelling words from the first column.

When Balaam was going with the princes of Moab, the donkey he was riding turned aside into a field. Next, the donkey crushed Balaam's foot against a wall. Balaam **(1)** _wondered_ what was going on. It was **(2)** _unlike_ his donkey to act like that. Soon the donkey fell down under him and spoke in a **(3)** _language_ that Balaam understood. The donkey asked Balaam a **(4)** _question_. Then God opened Balaam's eyes, and he saw an angel with a drawn sword. The angel told Balaam that his donkey had **(5)** _kept_ him from being killed. God was not pleased that Balaam was going with the princes of Moab (Numbers 22).

6. Write two sentences of your own. Use **unpainted** and **broken** in the first sentence. Use **wondered** and **tracks** in the second sentence.

a. _(Individual sentences.)_

b. _____

7. Which NEW WORDS have these meanings?

a. Not having its normal color.

discolored

b. Condition of the outside air.

weather

c. Six more than ten. _sixteen_

d. Not organized; untidy.

disorderly

e. Holiday for expressing special gratitude to God. _Thanksgiving_

13. *sixteen*   Who knows the first *sixteen* verses?
14. *question*   God asked Job a *question* about snow.
15. *quickly*   "Arise up *quickly*," the angel told Peter.
16. *broken*   The fish had not *broken* the net.

We *wondered* what animals made such large *tracks*.

Father *kept* his head covered as he *watched* the bees.

8. Each word below has more than one meaning. Complete each sentence with the word that fits best.

square   question   cracks   tracks

a. An asking sentence is a __question__ .

b. After the earthquake, there were many __cracks__ in the walls.

c. Draw all four sides equal to make a __square__ .

d. We tried to identify the animal __tracks__ .

e. William Penn carefully planned for Philadelphia to be laid out in large, __square__ city blocks.

f. When Glen forgets to remove his boots, he __tracks__ dirt onto the kitchen floor.

g. The teacher will __question__ Ella about her careless work.

h. A squirrel __cracks__ nuts with its teeth.

C. Building Words

C. 31 points

Verb Forms

1. Complete each sentence with the spelling word that is a form of the boldface verb.

a. **track**   Our dog __tracks__ rabbits.

b. **crack**   Some glass __cracks__ easily.

c. **check**   Arthur __checks__ his answers a second time.

d. **mix**   We __mixed__ the paint.

e. **waxed**   I helped Mother __wax__ the floor.

f. **watch**   The disciples __watched__ Jesus ascend.

g. **wonder**   Who __wondered__ where I am?

2. Use the boldface verbs to complete the sentences correctly.

break   broke   broken
keep   kept   kept

a. Everyone should __keep__ God's laws. Daniel __kept__ praying every day. David had __kept__ the sheep from harm.

b. Thieves cannot __break__ into heaven. The many large fish __broke__ the net. Paul's ship was __broken__ in the storm.

114

• **Prefixes and Suffixes**
A syllable added to the beginning of a word is a **prefix**. A syllable added to the end of a word is a **suffix**.

3. Which NEW WORDS have these meanings?

a. not painted ____unpainted____

b. not orderly ____disorderly____

4. In exercise 3, what prefixes are added to **painted** and **orderly** to make words that mean the opposite? _un-_ _dis-_

5. Use the prefix **un-** to build words with these meanings.

a. not mixed ____unmixed____

b. not like ____unlike____

c. not colored ____uncolored____

d. not waxed ____unwaxed____

6. Use the prefix **dis-** to build words with these meanings.

a. do opposite of **appear** ___disappear___

b. do opposite of **like** ____dislike____

c. do opposite of **obey** ____disobey____

d. do opposite of **agree** ____disagree____

7. Which spelling word has the root word **quick**? ____quickly____ What is the suffix in this word? _-ly_

8. The root word of **disorderly** is **order**. What prefix do you see in this word? _dis-_ What suffix do you see? _-ly_

Bible Thoughts

Use spelling words to complete these verses.

9. "He answered and said unto them, When it is evening, ye say, It will be fair ____weather____ : for the sky is red" (Matthew 16:2).

10. "Now when this was noised abroad, the multitude came together, and were confounded, because that every man heard them speak in his own ____language____ " (Acts 2:6).

LESSON 29

NEW WORDS

remove
which
yoke
youngest
salvation
gloves
twelve
golden

whistle
silver
discover
fearful
vacation
awhile
careful
wooden

REVIEW WORDS

whenever
yourself

visited
thankful

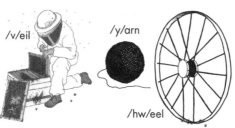

/v/eil   /y/arn

/hw/eel

3. Which NEW WORD ends with /v/ spelled **ve** and then the suffix **-s**?

_____gloves_____

4. Write the NEW WORDS that end with /v/ spelled **ve.**

_____remove_____   _____twelve_____

5. The /v/ sound in each word should be spelled **ve.** Write the words correctly.

sa/v/ _save_   dri/v/ _drive_

abo/v/ _above_   car/v/ _carve_

lea/v/ _leave_   ner/v/ _nerve_

A. Sounds and Letters

> • The /v/ sound is usually spelled **v**, except that at the end of a word it is usually spelled **ve.**
> **v̲eil sil̲v̲er twel̲v̲e glov̲e**

1. Write the spelling words that begin with /v/ spelled **v.**

_____vacation_____   _____visited_____

2. Write the spelling words that have /v/ spelled **v** within the word.

_____salvation_____   _____discover_____

_____silver_____   _____whenever_____

> • The /y/ sound at the beginning of a word is usually spelled **y.**
> **y̲arn   y̲oung**
> However, the /yo͞o/ sound is spelled **u.**   **u̲se   u̲nit**

6. Write three spelling words that begin with /y/.   _____yoke_____

_____youngest_____   _____yourself_____

7. The missing sound in each word is /y/ spelled **y.** Write the words correctly.

_ear _year_   law_er _lawyer_

_outh _youth_   can_on _canyon_

A. 39 points

116

Test Sentences

1. *wooden*   Rails are fastened to *wooden* ties.
2. *gloves*   This pair of *gloves* is made of wool.
3. *yoke*   The two oxen have a *yoke* around their necks.
4. *which*   Choose *which* Bible story we shall read.
5. *discover* A plumber could *discover* the trouble.
6. *awhile*   Sit down *awhile* until we are ready.
7. *fearful*   The broken glass was a *fearful* sight.
8. *remove*   Come in and *remove* your wraps.
9. *whistle*   A train *whistle* sounded nearby.
10. *vacation* During *vacation,* remember to read.
11. *careful* "Oh, be *careful,* little hands, what you do."
12. *silver*   God knew about the *silver* Achan stole.

8. The beginning sound in each word is /yōō/ spelled **u**. Write the words correctly.

_nit ____unit____   _sual ____usual____

> • **The consonant blend /hw/ is spelled wh.   wheel   awhile**

9. Write four spelling words that have /hw/.

_____which_____   _____awhile_____

_____whistle_____   _____whenever_____

10. Write the spelling words that end with **ful**.

_____fearful_____   _____thankful_____

_____careful_____

11. Which NEW WORDS end with /shən/ spelled **tion**?

_____salvation_____   _____vacation_____

Write spelling words for these phonetic spellings.

12. gōl′dən _____golden_____

13. wōōd′ən _____wooden_____

14. di skuv′ər _____discover_____

15. hwis′əl _____whistle_____

16. ri mōōv′ _____remove_____

17. ə hwīl′ _____awhile_____

B. Using Your Words

B. 23 points

Fill in the blanks with spelling words from the first column.

When Elijah called Elisha to follow him, Elisha was plowing with **(1)** ____twelve____

(2) ____yoke____ of oxen (1 Kings 19:19). These animals, **(3)** ____which____

were useful in Bible times, are still used today in some countries. They can pull carts

and wagons. When people butcher oxen, they **(4)** ____remove____ the hide and tan

it to make leather. The leather is used to make shoes, **(5)** ____gloves____, and other

things. The meat of oxen is good to eat. The bones, dung, and blood make good fertil-

izer. Even the horns may be made into combs and knife handles.

6. Write two sentences of your own. Use **careful** and **remove** in the first sentence. Use **thankful** and **visited** in the second sentence.

a. _____(Individual sentences.)_____

b. _____

117

13. *twelve*   Jacob had *twelve* sons.
14. *youngest*   David was Jesse's *youngest* son.
15. *golden*   The king held out his *golden* scepter.
16. *salvation*   Jesus brought *salvation* to mankind.

Do your work *yourself whenever* you can.

Our minister was *thankful* that we *visited* him.

7. Write the spelling word that sounds almost like **witch**. _____which_____ A woman who supposedly has magical powers is a _____witch_____ . To begin a question or to mean "what one," we use the word _____which_____ .

8. Use your answers to number 7 in the following sentences.

   a. Saul should not have gone to the _____witch_____ at En-dor for help.

   b. _____Which_____ way does the Nile River flow?

   c. Lynn knows _____which_____ way to turn at the crossroads.

9. Write the spelling word that fits with each group.

   a. biggest, smallest, oldest
   _____youngest_____

   b. conversion, redemption, deliverance
   _____salvation_____

   c. blow, puff, wheeze
   _____whistle_____

   d. gold, copper, iron
   _____silver_____

   e. holiday, rest, leisure
   _____vacation_____

   f. alert, watchful, diligent
   _____careful_____

   g. whatever, however, wherever
   _____whenever_____

   h. myself, himself, herself
   _____yourself_____

C. Building Words

Prefixes and Suffixes

1. Write the NEW WORD that has the prefix **dis-** and means "find for the first time."

   _____discover_____

2. Add the prefix **un-** to REVIEW WORDS to build words with the meanings given.

   not thankful _____unthankful_____

   not visited _____unvisited_____

3. Add **un-** to a NEW WORD to build a word that means "remove a yoke from."

   _____unyoke_____

4. Which NEW WORD has the prefix **re-**?

   _____remove_____

5. Add **re-** to a REVIEW WORD to build a word that means "visited again."

   _____revisited_____

C. 25 points

6. Add **re-** to the underlined words to build words with the meanings given.

a. <u>copy</u> again _____recopy_____

b. <u>order</u> again _____reorder_____

c. <u>load</u> again _____reload_____

d. <u>cross</u> again _____recross_____

e. <u>turn</u> back _____return_____

7. Write the spelling words that have these meanings.

a. full of thanks _____thankful_____

b. full of care _____careful_____

c. having fear _____fearful_____

8. What suffix in these words means "full of" or "having"? _-ful (Hyphen is optional.)_

9. Write the correct words by adding **-ful** to the underlined words.

a. "God loveth a [<u>cheer</u>] giver" (2 Corinthians 9:7). _____cheerful_____

b. The baby fell into a <u>peace</u> sleep.

_____peaceful_____

c. Honest people give <u>truth</u> answers.

_____truthful_____

d. The <u>color</u> rainbow reminds us of God's promise. _____colorful_____

10. Write the spelling words that have these meanings.

a. made of wood _____wooden_____

b. made of gold _____golden_____

11. What suffix means "made of"? _-en_

Bible Thoughts

Use spelling words to complete these verses.

12. "We ought not to think that the Godhead is like unto gold, or _____silver_____, or stone, graven by art and man's device" (Acts 17:29).

13. "Then the king held out the _____golden_____ sceptre toward Esther" (Esther 8:4).

14. "Therefore with joy shall ye draw water out of the wells of _____salvation_____" (Isaiah 12:3).

Lesson 30—91 points

LESSON 30

25	26	27	28	29
grown	noise	forgave	square	remove
since	desert	carrying	mixed	which
space	teeth	break	quickly	yoke
mercy	women	forgotten	language	youngest
chase	dozen	choose	question	salvation
absent	slept	pocketbook	sixteen	gloves
I'd	mouse	trunk	unlike	twelve
he'd	led	stockings	unpainted	golden
recess	wisdom	broke	wax	whistle
answer	children	skates	cracks	silver
blessing	hose	Christmas	weather	discover
lace	praise	pictures	broken	fearful
blew	easy	music	checks	vacation
crossed	presents	chickens	Thanksgiving	awhile
nurse	reasons	it's	disorderly	careful
cents	taught	we're	discolored	wooden

A. Sounds and Letters Review

A. 21 points

The symbol after each number shows what sound is missing in each of these spelling words. Write the words.

1. /j/ langua__ _____language_____

2. /s/ __ince mer__y cha__ ble__ing
_____since_____ _____chase_____
_____mercy_____ _____blessing_____

3. /z/ do__en ea__y prai__
_____dozen_____ _____praise_____
_____easy_____

4. /k/ yo__e trun__ __arrying sto__ings
_____yoke_____ _____carrying_____
_____trunk_____ _____stockings_____

5. /w/ __isdom _____wisdom_____

6. /ks/ wa__ cra__
_____wax_____ _____cracks_____

7. /kw/ s__are _____square_____

8. /v/ sil__er twel__
_____silver_____ _____twelve_____

9. /hw/ __istle _____whistle_____

Write spelling words for these.

10. myōō′zik _____music_____

11. vā kā′shən _____vacation_____

120

Review—Test Sentences

1. *remove* For a time, David would not *remove* the ark of God.
2. *cents* A man paid ten *cents* for an apple.
3. *mouse* The cat caught a *mouse* for dinner.
4. *wooden* Brooms have *wooden* handles.
5. *golden* We gazed at the *golden* sunset.
6. *it's* Yes, *it's* soon his birthday.
7. *unlike* It is *unlike* him to be frowning.
8. *children* Jesus loves the *children* dearly.
9. *twelve* Jesus chose *twelve* disciples.
10. *easy* "Knowledge is *easy* unto him that understandeth."
11. *space* Not much *space* is left.
12. *mixed* The cook *mixed* the sugar and flour.

B. Using Your Words Review

Complete this circle puzzle with spelling words from Lessons 25–29 to match the meanings. Print one letter in each space in the circle. The last letter of each word is the same as the first letter of the next word, so print that letter only once.

B. 12 points

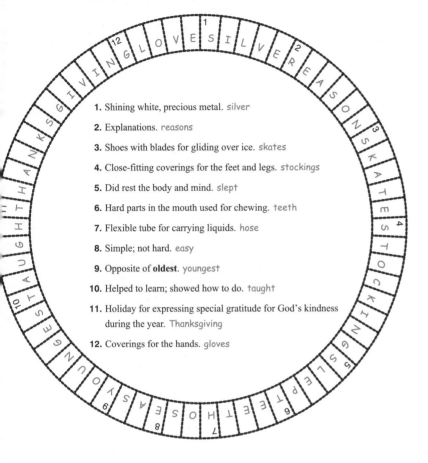

1. Shining white, precious metal. silver

2. Explanations. reasons

3. Shoes with blades for gliding over ice. skates

4. Close-fitting coverings for the feet and legs. stockings

5. Did rest the body and mind. slept

6. Hard parts in the mouth used for chewing. teeth

7. Flexible tube for carrying liquids. hose

8. Simple; not hard. easy

9. Opposite of **oldest**. youngest

10. Helped to learn; showed how to do. taught

11. Holiday for expressing special gratitude for God's kindness during the year. Thanksgiving

12. Coverings for the hands. gloves

121

13. *trunk*	Set the box into the *trunk,* please.
14. careful	Be careful as you spell.
15. *teeth*	We brush our *teeth* daily.
16. *chase*	Their turkey wanted to *chase* the chickens.
17. *awhile*	The baby slept *awhile* after dinner.
18. *pocketbook*	The girl's *pocketbook* is black.
19. *break*	Did the jar *break* when it fell?
20. *he'd*	We thought *he'd* be hurt.
21. *answer*	Say your *answer* loud and clear.
22. *music*	They learned a new song in *music* class.
23. *women*	Men, *women,* and children heard Ezra read.
24. *vacation*	Summer *vacation* will come soon.
25. *wisdom*	Jesus increased in *wisdom* and stature.

C. Building Words Review

1. Decide whether the boldface word is plural or shows possession. Spell it correctly with **-s** or **-'s**.

Chicken/z/ have red combs.

_____chickens_____

A **chicken/z/** comb is on top of its head.

_____chicken's_____

Many **nurs/iz/** use Celsius thermometers.

_____nurses_____

Betty tried to read the **nurse/iz/** thermometer. _____nurse's_____

2. Write these proper nouns and number sentences. Abbreviate the underlined words.

Tenth <u>Street</u>	Tenth St.
Willow <u>Road</u>	Willow Rd.
Fourth <u>Avenue</u>	Fourth Ave.
1 <u>yard</u> = 36 <u>inches</u>	1 yd. = 36 in.
1 <u>mile</u> = 5,280 <u>feet</u>	1 mi. = 5,280 ft.
1 <u>month</u> = 4 <u>weeks</u>	1 mo. = 4 wk.

3. Begin each sentence with the contraction made from the boldface word and **not**. Remember to use capital letters.

were _Weren't_ the people rising?

have _Haven't_ the prices risen?

should _Shouldn't_ the balloon rise?

can _Can't_ the bread rise?

will _Won't_ the sun rise soon?

4. Write the correct word in each blank.

its, it's A dog wags _____its_____ tail when _____it's_____ happy.

your, you're This is where _____you're_____ to put _____your_____ boots.

their, they're Cows often chew _____their_____ cud when _____they're_____ lying down.

5. Write contractions for these words.

I would _____I'd_____ she is _____she's_____

he had _____he'd_____ we are _____we're_____

6. Complete each sentence with a spelling word that is a form of the boldface verb.

a. **sleep** Frieda has _____slept_____ a long time.

b. **grow** The calves have _____grown_____ bigger.

c. **choose** Abram allowed Lot to _____choose_____ first.

d. **forget** We have not _____forgotten_____ .

e. **lead** Melvin _____led_____ the singing.

f. **forgive** Jesus _____forgave_____ His enemies.

g. **break** Can you _____break_____ this stick?

h. **break** Who _____broke_____ Carolyn's pencil?

C. 58 points

2. Allow 2 points per number sentence.

26.	_Christmas_	December 25 is _Christma_s Day.
27.	_reasons_	He wrote two _reasons_ for the change.
28.	_youngest_	Someone must be the _youngest_ child.
29.	_led_	One man _led_ the way.
30.	_gloves_	Are both your _gloves_ wet?
31.	_crossed_	The Israelites _crossed_ the Jordan river.
32.	_since_	Two months passed _since_ it happened.
33.	_dozen_	I purchased one _dozen_ eggs.
34.	_pictures_	Children like _pictures_ of animals.
35.	_silver_	Some men work in the _silver_ mine.
36.	_skates_	The ice _skates_ are in the attic.
37.	_carrying_	The mother cat is _carrying_ her kitten.
38.	_absent_	Several were _absent_ that day.

i. **break**   Laura has ___broken___ her arm.

j. **blow**   The wind ___blew___ all night.

7. Write the plurals of the underlined nouns.

a <u>present</u>   several ___presents___

one <u>tooth</u>   all my ___teeth___

this <u>woman</u>   these ___women___

every <u>recess</u>   many ___recesses___

one <u>glove</u>   both ___gloves___

one <u>child</u>   several ___children___

8. Use **un-** to build words with these meanings.

not <u>painted</u>   ___unpainted___

opposite of <u>crossed</u>   ___uncrossed___

9. Use **dis-** to build words with these meanings.

not <u>orderly</u>   ___disorderly___

opposite of <u>like</u>   ___dislike___

10. Use **re-** to build words with these meanings.

<u>crossed</u> again   ___recrossed___

<u>order</u> again   ___reorder___

11. Use **-er** to build words with these meanings.

person who <u>skates</u>   ___skater___

thing that <u>mixes</u>   ___mixer___

12. Use **-ful** to build words with these meanings.

having <u>fear</u>   ___fearful___

full of <u>care</u>   ___careful___

13. Use **-en** to build words with these meanings.

made of <u>wood</u>   ___wooden___

made of <u>gold</u>   ___golden___

Bible Thoughts

Use spelling words to complete these verses.

14. "But Thomas, one of the ___twelve___, called Didymus, was not with them when Jesus came" (John 20:24).

15. "Take my ___yoke___ upon you, and learn of me; for I am meek and lowly in heart: and ye shall find rest unto your souls" (Matthew 11:29).

39. *presents*   Some gave *presents* to the sick boy.
40. *checks*   Father writes *checks* to pay the bills.
41. *taught*   Jesus *taught* many people.
42. *unpainted*   Arnold bought an *unpainte*d chair.
43. *praise*   I will *praise* the Lord.
44. *mercy*   "Surely goodness and *mercy* shall follow me."
45. *forgotten*   Has anyone *forgotten* anything?
46. *square*   Everything fit into the *square* box.
47. *we're*   I believe *we're* nearly finished.
48. *disorderly*   No one likes a *disorder*ly room.
49. *discolored*   Light *discolor*ed the curtains.
50. *whistle*   The engineer blew his *whistle* loud.

LESSON 31

NEW WORDS

building
built
beginning
geography
enough
guess
calves
o'clock

flood
elephant
laughed
hungry
handkerchief
centimeter cm
meter m
kilometer km

REVIEW WORDS

stories
heaven

shining
aren't

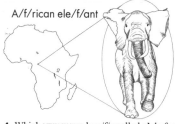

A/f/rican ele/f/ant

4. Which NEW WORD has /f/ spelled **gh** before the suffix **-ed**? _____laughed_____

5. Write two spelling words that have /f/ spelled **ph**.

_____geography_____   _____elephant_____

6. Which REVIEW WORD has /e/ spelled **ea**?

_____heaven_____

7. Write **kilometer**. _____kilometer_____

Find its two pronunciations in the Speller Dictionary. When **kilometer** is accented on **kil**, what sound does the **o** have? /ə / When it is accented on **lom**, what sound does the **o** have? /o /

8. Write the spelling word that ends with /s/ spelled **ss**. _____guess_____

9. Write the spelling word that ends with /k/ spelled **ck**. _____o'clock_____

10. Write the spelling word that begins with /s/ spelled **c**. _____centimeter_____

Now write the spelling word that begins with /k/ spelled **c**. _____calves_____

A. Sounds and Letters

> • The /f/ sound is usually spelled **f** or **ff**.   **four   puff**
> Sometimes /f/ is spelled **gh** or **ph**.
>   **tough   laugh**
>   **phonetic   elephant**

1. Which NEW WORD begins with /f/ spelled **f**?

_____flood_____

2. Which NEW WORD ends with /f/ spelled **f**?

_____handkerchief_____

3. Which NEW WORD ends with /f/ spelled **gh**?

_____enough_____

A. 20 points

Test Sentences

1. *flood*	During the *Flood,* Noah was safe.
2. *built*	Solomon *built* the first temple.
3. *beginning*	"In the *beginning* was the Word."
4. *enough*	The boy's lunch was *enough* for everyone.
5. *o'clock*	From four to six *o'clock* is two hours.
6. *building*	That high *building* is a skyscraper.
7. *geography*	We study land in *geography* class.
8. *elephant*	An African *elephant* has large ears.
9. *guess*	Is my *guess* right?
10. *handkerchief*	Fold a *handkerchief* neatly.
11. *laughed*	The baby *laughed* when she saw the toy.
12. *hungry*	We fed the *hungry* dog.

Write spelling words for these phonetic spellings.

11. haŋ′kər chif _____handkerchief_____

12. ges _____guess_____

13. bil′ding _____building_____

14. i nuf′ _____enough_____

15. When **hunger** is changed to **hungry**, the letter **e** is dropped. Write both words.

_____hunger_____   _____hungry_____

B. Using Your Words

B. 15 points

Fill in the blanks with spelling words from the first column.

In 1608 a glass plant was **(1)** _____built_____ at Jamestown, Virginia. Since then, more glass plants have been started, as the uses of glass increased. There are many different kinds of glass. Windows are made from flat glass. Car windows are made from safety glass, which is strong **(2)** _____enough_____ so that it will not break easily. Glass building blocks may be seen in a tall apartment **(3)** _____building_____ or factory. Think of how strong the blocks must be for a building that is ten or eleven **(4)** _____stories_____ high. Can you **(5)** _____guess_____ what is used to make fluffy insulation for houses? It is made from a glass product called fiberglass.

6. Write two sentences of your own. Use **shining** and **o'clock** in the first sentence. Use **calves** and **hungry** in the second sentence.

a. _____(Individual sentences.)_____

b. _____

7. What are these people saying? Fill in the blanks with spelling words.

a. Isn't that _____elephant_____ huge?

b. I will quickly shut the gate before the _____calves_____ get out.

c. The smell of this pie is making me _____hungry_____.

d. We learned about this river in _____geography_____ class.

125

13. *calves*   Simon feeds the *calves* before breakfast.

For numbers 14–16, write the word *and* its abbreviation.
14. *centimeter*   *cm*   A pen is a *centimeter* thick.
15. *meter*   *m*   A *meter* stick is longer than a yardstick.
16. *kilometer*   *km*   A *kilometer* is a thousand meters.

I like to read *stories* of *heaven*.

Aren't any stars *shining?*

e. Look, this bug is one ____centimeter____ long.

f. The angels said that Jesus will return from ____heaven____ in the same way He left.

C. Building Words

meter	centimeter
m	cm

1,000 meters = 1 kilometer

____1,000 m = 1 km____

C. 39 points

Abbreviations

1. In Lesson 21, you studied the abbreviations for **inch**, **foot**, **yard**, and **mile**. Write those abbreviations.

____in.____   ____yd.____

____ft.____   ____mi.____

2. The abbreviations in this lesson are for metric measures. These abbreviations end (with, <u>without</u>) periods.

3. Write the abbreviation that stands for **centimeter** or **centimeters**.

____cm____

4. Write the abbreviation that stands for **meter** or **meters**.

____m____

5. Write the abbreviation that stands for **kilometer** or **kilometers**.

____km____

6. Write these number sentences, using abbreviations.

100 centimeters = 1 meter

____100 cm = 1 m____

> • **Plural and Possessive Nouns**
> To form the plurals of some nouns that end with **f**, change the **f** to **v** and add **-es.**
> **half—halves**   **leaf—leaves**

7. a. Write the spelling word in which **f** was changed to **v** to make it plural. Then write its singular form.

____calves____   ____calf____

b. To make **handkerchief** plural, simply add **s.** ____handkerchiefs____

8. Look at the words you wrote for number 7. In which one is final **f** not changed to **v** before adding **s**?

____handkerchiefs____

9. Build plural nouns by adding **-s** or **-es** to these singular nouns.

| **flood** | **building** | **elephant** |
| **guess** | **centimeter** | **handkerchief** |

____floods____	____guesses____
____buildings____	____centimeters____
____elephants____	____handkerchiefs____

6. Allow 2 points per number sentence.

10. Which spelling word was made plural by changing **y** to **i** and adding **-es**?

    stories

11. Write these phrases a short way by using possessive nouns.

the den belonging to a wolf

    a wolf's den

the trunk the elephant has

    the elephant's trunk

the legs of the calf

    the calf's legs

the book owned by my teacher

    my teacher's book

12. Write the spelling words that are **-ing** forms of **begin** and **shine**.

    beginning   _shining_

In which word did you double the final consonant? _beginning_

In which word did you drop the final **e**?

    shining

Contractions

13. Write the spelling words that are contractions for these phrases.

are not _aren't_

of the clock _o'clock_

14. Rewrite each phrase, using the contraction for **of the clock**.

two of the clock _two o'clock_

eight of the clock _eight o'clock_

four of the clock _four o'clock_

Bible Thoughts

Use spelling words that are forms of *build* to complete these sentences. Write one word twice.

15. Noah was _building_ the ark for many years. He _built_ it exactly as God told him. Noah was safe in the ark after it was _built_.

LESSON 32

NEW WORDS

bicycle   fruit
owner   suit
juice   fields
beautiful   peas
sleepy   suddenly
received   liter l
chief   gram g
believe   kilogram kg

REVIEW WORDS

piece   greatest
later   thinner

A. Sounds and Letters

> • **I before e, except after c,**
> or when sounded like /ā/
> as in **neighbor** and **weigh**.

1. Which spelling words have /ē/ spelled **ie**?

_____chief_____   _____fields_____

_____believe_____   _____piece_____

Does the /ē/ sound come immediately after

c in any word you wrote? _____no_____

2. Which spelling word has /ē/ spelled **ei**?

_____received_____ Does /ē/ come imme-

diately after **c** in this word? _____yes_____

Jeffr/ē/ r/ō/d
his bl/o͞o/
b/ī/cycle to
the m/ā/lbox.

3. Which spelling word has both an /ī/ sound

and an /i/ sound? _____bicycle_____

Which letter spells /ī/ ? __i__ Which let-

ter spells /i/? __y__

Cycle comes from a Greek word that means
"circle," and **bi-** means "two." Think **bi
cycle** as you write the word again.

_____bicycle_____

4. Write the NEW WORD that rhymes with

heater. _____liter_____

What letter spells /ē/? __i__

5. Write the NEW WORD that begins with /ō/.

_____owner_____ What two letters spell

/ō/? __ow__

6. Which NEW WORD has /yo͞o/ spelled **eau**?

_____beautiful_____

7. Which NEW WORDS have /o͞o/?

_____juice_____   _____suit_____

_____fruit_____

What letters spell /o͞o/ in each of these

words? __ui__

8. Which NEW WORD has three syllables and

ends with **gram**? _____kilogram_____

What letter spells /ə/ in this word? __o__

A. 28 points

128

Test Sentences

1.	*sleepy*	When I am *sleepy,* I cannot work well.
2.	*bicycle*	Roger must pump up the *bicycle* tire.
3.	*juice*	Orange *juice* is good to drink.
4.	*fields*	Many *fields* were planted by hand in Bible times.
5.	*owner*	Who is the *owner* of this lunch box?
6.	*beautiful*	Adam and Eve saw *beautiful* fruit.
7.	*suit*	Yes, it will *suit* us to make sandwiches.
8.	*peas*	We often eat *peas* and carrots mixed.
9.	*fruit*	How many *fruit* trees are in his orchard?
10.	*believe*	We *believe* that Jesus rose again.
11.	*chief*	The *chief* butler forgot about Joseph.
12.	*received*	"Freely ye have *received,* freely give."

9. Which spelling word has the /th/ sound?

_____thinner_____

Write spelling words for these phonetic spellings.

10. pēz _____peas_____

11. slē′pē _____sleepy_____

12. sud′ən lē _____suddenly_____

13. grā′tist _____greatest_____

14. pēs _____piece_____

B. 15 points

B. Using Your Words

Fill in the blanks with spelling words from the first column.

Glass is made in somewhat the same way that your mother makes hard candy. For glass, the **(1)** _____chief_____ material is sand. Sand, lime, and soda are heated until the mixture is a thin liquid almost like **(2)** _____juice_____. One method of shaping glass is blowing. A long **(3)** _____piece_____ of hollow iron called a blowpipe is dipped into melted glass. A small amount of melted glass sticks to the end of the blowpipe. The workman blows gently until a bubble appears. He may squeeze and twirl this bubble to make a **(4)** _____beautiful_____ vase. The red-hot glass is **(5)** _____later_____ broken from the blowpipe and allowed to cool slowly.

6. Write two sentences of your own. Use **piece** and **thinner** in the first sentence. Use **suddenly** and **chief** in the second sentence.

a. _____(Individual sentences.)_____

b. _____

7. What are these people saying? Fill in the blanks with spelling words.

a. Most of my _____fields_____ have already been plowed.

b. I will gladly help you weed the _____peas_____.

c. There is about a _____liter_____ of water in this watering can.

d. A nickel weighs more than one _____gram_____.

129

13. *suddenly*   Light *suddenly* shone in the prison.

For numbers 14–16, write the word *and* its abbreviation.
14. *liter*   *l*   One *liter* is ten deciliters.
15. *gram*   *g*   One *gram* is ten decigrams.
16. *kilogram*   *kg*   One *kilogram* is a thousand grams.

The *greatest* need cannot wait until *later*.

Is your *piece* of paper *thinner* than his?

e. This inner tube for my
___bicycle___ tire must
be repaired.

 f. I am sewing a dark blue
___suit___ for Father.

C. Building Words

C. 41 points

> • **Words That Compare**
> Longer words compare by using
> the words **more** and **most** rather
> than the suffixes **-er** and **-est**.
> **beautiful, more beautiful,
> most beautiful**

1. Add **-er** and **-est** to the following words.
Drop the final **e**, double the consonant, or
change **y** to **i** as needed.

great	greater	greatest
late	later	latest
thin	thinner	thinnest
sleepy	sleepier	sleepiest
juicy	juicier	juiciest

2. Complete these sentences by using **more**
and **most** with the underlined words.

a. A cheerful smile makes a face <u>beautiful</u>.
The sunrise this morning seemed
___more___ ___beautiful___ than the one
yesterday.
Esther thinks pansies are the ___most___
___beautiful___ flowers of all.

b. The wind <u>suddenly</u> blew my papers.
The car might stop ___more___
___suddenly___ than you expect.
This storm came the ___most___
___suddenly___ of any that I remember.

> • **Good** and **bad** do not compare
> by using **-er** and **-est** or **more**
> and **most**.
> **good, better, best
> bad, worse, worst**

3. Complete these sentences with **good**, **better**, and **best**.
Brenda thinks apple pie is ___good___. I
think cherry pie is ___better___. Elmer
thinks lemon pie is the ___best___ kind.

4. Complete these sentences with **bad**, **worse**,
and **worst**.
My sore leg felt ___bad___ last week.
Yesterday it felt ___worse___ than it had the
day before. Today it feels the ___worst___
of all.

Abbreviations

5. Write the abbreviation for **liter** or **liters**.

_____l_____

6. Write the abbreviation for **gram** or **grams**.

_____g_____

7. Write the abbreviation for **kilogram** or **kilo-grams**. _____kg_____

8. Write these number sentences, using abbreviations. Use the abbreviation **cl** for **centiliters**.

100 centiliters = 1 liter _____100 cl = 1 l_____

1,000 grams = 1 kilogram _____1,000 g = 1 kg_____

Prefixes and Suffixes

9. Complete these sentences with words made by adding **-ful** to **fruit** and **beauty**.

In **beauty**, you will change the **y** to what letter? ___i___

The orchard was _____fruitful_____ last summer.

We watched the _____beautiful_____ sunset until it faded.

10. Complete these sentences with words made by adding **-er** to **receive**, **own**, and **sleep**.

After a man sells something, he is no longer the _____owner_____ of it.

When someone gives you something, you are a _____receiver_____.

The captain said to Jonah, "What meanest thou, O _____sleeper_____? arise, call upon thy God."

11. Use **-er** and **un-** to build a word that means "a person who does not believe."

_____unbeliever_____

12. What words can you build by adding **-ly** to **sudden** and **chief**?

_____suddenly_____ _____chiefly_____

13. What words can you build by adding **-y** to **sleep** and **juice**? In **juice**, you will drop what letter? ___e___

_____sleepy_____ _____juicy_____

Bible Thoughts

Use spelling words to complete these sentences.

14. While Jesus was praying, Peter, James, and John became very _____sleepy_____ (Matthew 26: 37, 43).

15. "Whosoever therefore shall humble himself as this little child, the same is _____greatest_____ in the kingdom of heaven" (Matthew 18:4).

8. Allow 2 points per number sentence.

131

LESSON 33

NEW WORDS

tomorrow   good-bye
poem   great-grandmother
downstairs   great-uncle
cookbook   terrible
mountains   curve
against   ounce oz.
pint pt.   gallon gal.
quart qt.   pound lb.

REVIEW WORDS

pictures   Mennonite
painting   scare

good-bye

A. Sounds and Letters

1. Which spelling word has

/âr/ spelled **air**? _downstairs_

/âr/ spelled **are**? _scare_

2. Which spelling word has

/ôr/ spelled **orr**? _tomorrow_

/ôr/ spelled **ar** after **qu**? _quart_

3. Which spelling word has

/ûr/ spelled **ur**? _curve_

/er/ spelled **err**? _terrible_

4. Which NEW WORDS have /o͞o/ spelled **oo**?

cookbook _good-bye_

5. In which NEW WORDS do you hear /ou/?

downstairs _ounce_
mountains _pound_

6. In the words below, the missing letters spell /ə/. Write the words correctly.

gall__n pict__res Menn__nite
terr__ble t__morrow po__m

gallon _tomorrow_
terrible _Mennonite_
pictures _poem_

7. Which spelling word begins with /ə/?

against What two letters spell /e/

in this word? _ai_

8. Which REVIEW WORD has

/ā/ spelled **ai**? _painting_

/chûr/ spelled **ture**? _pictures_

9. Which NEW WORDS have /ā/ spelled **ea**?

great-grandmother _great-uncle_

10. Write the one-syllable NEW WORD that has

the /ī/ sound. _pint_

11. Which NEW WORD ends with

the /ī/ sound? _good-bye_

the /ō/ sound? _tomorrow_

A. 38 points

132

Test Sentences

1. *curve* — The road makes a *curve* around the hill.
2. *great-uncle* — My *great-uncle* makes chairs.
3. *poem* — A *poem* is written by a poet.
4. *cookbook* — Which *cookbook* has the recipe?
5. *tomorrow* — God will care for us *tomorrow* too.
6. *downstairs* — We went *downstairs* quietly.
7. *good-bye* — Rhoda waved *good-bye* from the window.
8. *great-grandmother* — She is my *great-grandmother*.
9. *terrible* — Some lands had a *terrible* famine.
10. *mountains* — How many *mountains* can you name?
11. *against* — Prop the ladder *against* the house.

12. Which spelling words end with an **e** that is not sounded?

good-bye   ounce

terrible   Mennonite

curve   scare

Write spelling words for these phonetic spellings.

13. pō′əm   poem

14. kûrv   curve

15. pīnt   pint

16. ə genst′   against

17. ouns   ounce

B. Using Your Words

B. 15 points

Fill in the blanks with spelling words from the first column.

Do you know how a glass dish is decorated? One way is by sandblasting. First, pictures are cut out of a sheet of rubber. Then the rubber sheet is stuck to the glass dish. After that, grains of sand are shot **(1)** _against_ the dish. The sand nicks any part of the dish that is not covered with rubber. When the rubber sheet is removed, **(2)** _pictures_ made by the sand nicks can be seen.

Another way of decorating a glass dish is by **(3)** _painting_ it by hand. After the dish is painted, it is heated to make the paint dry and hard.

You have probably seen **(4)** _pint_ or **(5)** _quart_ canning jars with letters or designs on the outside. Such decorations are made when the jar is molded.

6. Write two sentences of your own. Use **cookbook** and **pictures** in the first sentence. Use **good-bye** and **great-grandmother** in the second sentence.

a. _____(Individual sentences.)_____

b. _____

7. What are these people saying? Fill in the blanks with spelling words.

a. Today is Thursday, and _tomorrow_ is Friday.

b. Slow down for the _curve_.

133

For numbers 12–16, write the word *and* its abbreviation.

12. *pint*   *pt.*   One *pint* equals two cups.
13. *quart*   *qt.*   One *quart* equals two pints.
14. *ounce*   *oz.*   An *ounce* of water is about two tablespoons.
15. *gallon*   *gal.*   One *gallon* equals four quarts.
16. *pound*   *lb.*   One *pound* is sixteen ounces.

Those *pictures* may *scare* Ezra.

The men were *painting* the *Mennonite* church.

c. I need one more

_____ounce_____ to make a pound.

d. In about fifteen minutes we will be at the Bernville _____Mennonite_____ Church.

 e. I will wait so that I do not _____scare_____ the baby.

f. Now I must say _____good-bye_____ .

C. Building Words

C. 33 points

- **Compound Words**
  In some compound words, the parts are joined by hyphens.
  good-bye
  Use a hyphen after **great** in names of relatives.
  great-grandmother

1. Most compound words are joined together as one word, like **sunshine**. Which spelling words are compounds made by joining **down** and **book** to other words?

_____downstairs_____ _____cookbook_____

2. Which spelling words are compounds with the parts joined by hyphens?

_____good-bye_____ _____great-uncle_____

_____great-grandmother_____

3. Build compound words by joining **great** to **grandfather** and **aunt**. Be sure to follow the rule.

_____great-grandfather_____ _____great-aunt_____

4. Build more compound words by using hyphens to join the following words.

half moon _____half-moon_____

foot pound _____foot-pound_____

full size _____full-size_____

Abbreviations

5. Write the abbreviations for these words.

ounce or **ounces** _____oz._____

pint or **pints** _____pt._____

quart or **quarts** _____qt._____

gallon or **gallons** _____gal._____

pound or **pounds** _____lb._____

6. The abbreviations above end (<u>with</u>, without) periods.

7. Write these number sentences, using abbreviations.

16 ounces = 1 pint _____16 oz. = 1 pt._____

2 pints = 1 quart _____2 pt. = 1 qt._____

7. Allow 2 points per number sentence.

4 quarts = 1 gallon   _4 qt. = 1 gal._

16 ounces = 1 pound   _16 oz. = 1 lb._

8. How may you write **gallon** on a shopping

list or a math paper? _____ _gal._ _____

How should you write **gallon** in a letter?

_____ _gallon_ _____

Syllables

9. Write the words below, and use slashes to
divide them into syllables according to the
VC/CV pattern.

mountains _____ _moun/tains_ _____

pictures _____ _pic/tures_ _____

10. Write **uncle**, and put a slash between the
syllables. Keep another consonant with **le**.

_____ _un/cle_ _____

11. Write **terrible**, and use slashes to divide the
syllables. Follow the VC/CV pattern and
the **le** pattern.

_____ _ter/ri/ble_ _____

12. Write **poem**, and divide it into syllables
between the two vowels. _____ _po/em_ _____

Bible Thoughts

**Use spelling words to
complete these sentences.**

13. The flood in Noah's day covered even the

_____ _mountains_ _____ (Genesis 7:20).

14. "If God be for us, who can be _____ _against_

us?" (Romans 8:31).

LESSON 34

31	32	33
building	bicycle	tomorrow
built	owner	poem
beginning	juice	downstairs
geography	beautiful	cookbook
enough	sleepy	mountains
guess	received	against
calves	chief	pint pt.
o'clock	believe	quart qt.
flood	fruit	good-bye
elephant	suit	great-grandmother
laughed	fields	great-uncle
hungry	peas	terrible
handkerchief	suddenly	curve
centimeter cm	liter l	ounce oz.
meter m	gram g	gallon gal.
kilometer km	kilogram kg	pound lb.

A. Sounds and Letters Review

A. 41 points

In exercises 1–9, the symbol at the beginning of each group shows what sound is missing. Write the words correctly. Use the Speller Dictionary if you need help.

1. /s/ again__t bi__ycle cha__e oun__e gue__

   against   ounce

   bicycle   guess

   chase

2. /z/ do__en pre__ents si__e ho__e

   dozen   size

   presents   hose

3. /w/ __ooden ____ wooden ____

4. /kw/ __art ____ quart ____

5. /k/ __ilometer __alves o'__lo__

   kilometer   o'clock

   calves

6. /ks/ mi__ed cra__

   mixed   cracks

7. /v/ sil__er cur__

   silver   curve

8. /y/ __oungest ____ youngest ____

9. /hw/ __istle ____ whistle ____

Review—Test Sentences

1.	*cookbook*	Which *cookbook* has the salad recipe?
2.	*good-bye*	The boys waved *good-bye* a long time.
3.	*o'clock*	A whistle blew at twelve *o'clock* noon.
4.	*pound*	"Thy *pound* hath gained ten pounds."
5.	*great-uncle*	Is your *great-uncle* living?
6.	*suit*	Jesus' teachings did not *suit* the Pharisees.
7.	*downstairs*	She tiptoed *downstairs* quietly.
8.	*fruit*	"A good tree bringeth forth good *fruit*."
9.	*peas*	We like *peas* with browned butter.
10.	*sleepy*	Who is *sleepy* today?
11.	*guess*	No one could *guess* the name.
12.	*chief*	Columbus is a *chief* city in Ohio.

10. Write words from Lesson 31 that have these sounds.

/a/ spelled **au** _____laughed_____

/e/ spelled **ue** _____guess_____

/i/ spelled **ui**

_____building_____ _____built_____

/f/ spelled **ph**

_____geography_____ _____elephant_____

11. Write words from Lesson 32 that have these sounds.

/o͞o/ spelled **ui** _____juice_____

_____fruit_____ _____suit_____

/yo͞o/ spelled **eau** _____beautiful_____

/ē/ spelled **i** _____liter_____

/ē/ spelled **ie** _____chief_____

_____believe_____ _____fields_____

/ē/ spelled **ei** _____received_____

12. Which word in Lesson 31 has **ie**?

_____handkerchief_____

13. In exercises 11 and 12, look at your answers that have **ie** or **ei**. They follow the rule that the letter __i__ comes before __e__ except after __c__.

14. Look at each set of boldface words below. Then underline the correct answers.

a. **staff bell pass buzz**
At the end of a one-syllable word with a short vowel sound, /f/, /l/, /s/, and /z/ are usually spelled with (single, <u>double</u>) letters.

b. **black check pick broke**
At the end of a one-syllable word with a short vowel sound, /k/ is usually spelled (c, <u>ck</u>, k, ke).

137

13. *laughed*   Sarah *laughed* at the angel's message.
14. *ounce*   This bottle holds half an *ounce* of glue.
15. *beautiful*   Spring is a *beautiful* season.
16. *fields*   Wheat *fields* are turning green.
17. *curve*   The path makes a *curve* around the rock.
18. *mountains*   Those *mountains* have snow on them.
19. *against*   Do not lean *against* the car.
20. *calves*   Three *calves* stood beside the fence.
21. *suddenly*   The engine *suddenly* stopped running.
22. *built*   Solomon *built* the temple.
23. *building*   What a magnificent *building* it was!
24. *hungry*   Jesus fed the *hungry* multitude.
25. *quart*   Only one *quart* of oil is left.
26. *owner*   The *owner* has the key.

B. Using Your Words Review

Complete this horseshoe puzzle with spelling words from Lessons 31–33 to match the meanings. Print one letter in each space in the horseshoe. The last letter of each word is the same as the first letter of the next word, so print that letter only once.

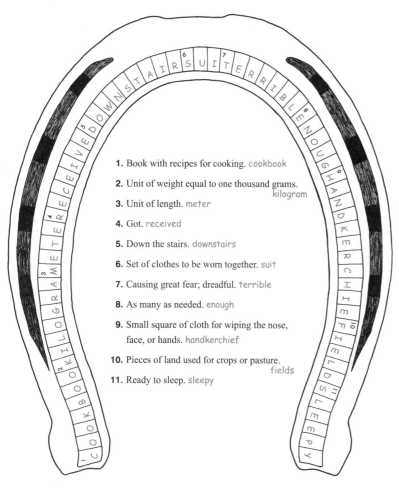

1. Book with recipes for cooking. cookbook

2. Unit of weight equal to one thousand grams. kilogram

3. Unit of length. meter

4. Got. received

5. Down the stairs. downstairs

6. Set of clothes to be worn together. suit

7. Causing great fear; dreadful. terrible

8. As many as needed. enough

9. Small square of cloth for wiping the nose, face, or hands. handkerchief

10. Pieces of land used for crops or pasture. fields

11. Ready to sleep. sleepy

27. *gallon*	Mother bought a *gallon* of milk.
28. *tomorrow*	Tonight or *tomorrow* it may rain.
29. *enough*	One pie is *enough* for dinner.
30. *flood*	Noah's family was saved from the *Flood*.
31. *poem*	The teacher read a *poem* about diligence.
32. geography	Have you studied Bible lands *geography?*
33. *beginning*	Read the *beginning* of the story.
34. *received*	We have *received* many blessings.
35. *bicycle*	Someone left his *bicycle* outside.
36. *pint*	The recipe calls for a *pint* of cream.
37. *kilogram*	The box holds a *kilogram* of rice.
38. *gram*	One *gram* of water is not very heavy.
39. *liter*	This bottle holds a *liter* of milk.
40. *kilometer*	Sally walks a *kilometer* to church.

C. Building Words Review

1. Write these number sentences, using abbreviations.

1 meter = 100 centimeters

___1 m = 100 cm___

1 kilometer = 1,000 meters

___1 km = 1,000 m___

1 kilogram = 1,000 grams

___1 kg = 1,000 g___

1 pound = 16 ounces ___1 lb. = 16 oz.___

1 quart = 2 pints ___1 qt. = 2 pt.___

1 gallon = 4 quarts ___1 gal. = 4 qt.___

2. The contraction for **of the clock** is

___o'clock___.

3. Write the plural form of **calf**.

___calves___

4. Write the Lesson 31 word in which the final consonant is doubled to add **-ing**.

___beginning___

5. Build compound words by matching the words in the first column to the words in the second column.

down   bye   ___downstairs___

cook   stairs   ___cookbook___

good   book   ___good-bye___

6. Build compound words by joining **great** to **uncle** and **grandmother**.

great-uncle   _great-grandmother_

7. Write **meter** and the spelling words that have prefixes added to **meter**.

___meter___   ___kilometer___

___centimeter___

8. Write **gram** and the spelling word that has a prefix added to **gram**.

___gram___   ___kilogram___

9. Write each word and the number of syllables in it.

terrible   ___terrible___   ___3___

flood   ___flood___   ___1___

hungry   ___hungry___   ___2___

tomorrow   ___tomorrow___   ___3___

poem   ___poem___   ___2___

10. Use slashes to divide the words into syllables by the patterns given.

VC/CV   **gallon**   **mountains**

___gal/lon___   ___moun/tains___

V/CV   **receive**   **liter**

___re/ceive___   ___li/ter___

Bible Thoughts

Use spelling words to complete these sentences.

11. "For he satisfieth the longing soul, and filleth the ___hungry___ soul with goodness" (Psalm 107:9).

12. Jesus told Jairus, "Be not afraid, only ___believe___" (Mark 5:36)

139

C. 41 points

1. Allow 2 points per number sentence.

41. *meter*   Mother bought a *meter* of apron material.

For numbers 42–50, write *only* the abbreviations of the words.

42. *lb.*   (*pound*)   Sixteen ounces are in a *pound*.

For numbers 42–50, write only the abbreviations.

43. *gal.*   (*gallon*)   Four quarts are in a *gallon*.

44. *oz.*   (*ounce*)   A pound is more than an *ounce*.

45. *qt.*   (*quart*)   A gallon is more than a *quart*.

Remember, we are writing abbreviations.

46. *g*   (*gram*)   Two paper clips weigh one *gram*.

47. *l*   (*liter*)   Gasoline is measured by the *liter*.

48. *cm*   (*centimeter*)   A large paper clip is one *centimeter* wide.

49. *m*   (*meter*)   Four books laid end to end measure one *meter*.

50. *km*   (*kilometer*)   Distance between cities is measured in *kilometers*.

Final Test

1.	*west*	The sun sets in the *west* each night.
2.	*body*	The sick boy's *body* is very weak.
3.	*bench*	This *bench* is so slippery.
4.	*roots*	The fig tree dried up from the *roots*.
5.	*ladder*	One rung of the *ladder* is broken.
6.	*heap*	The feed bags are on a *heap* on the floor.
7.	*branches*	He trimmed *branches* in the orchard.
8.	*stories*	Lois read two *stories* aloud.
9.	*becomes*	As water freezes, it *becomes* ice.
10.	*wanted*	The dog *wanted* another bone.
11.	*health*	We thank God for *health* and strength.
12.	*ordered*	Mother has *ordered* new shoes.
13.	*instead*	We ate crackers *instead* of bread.
14.	*heaven*	Jesus looked to *heaven* and prayed.
15.	*shipped*	Grain is *shipped* across the ocean.
16.	*Saturday*	One *Saturday* it rained.
17.	*later*	We ate *later* than usual.
18.	*schoolhouse*	The *schoolhouse* will be empty.
19.	*robin*	A young *robin* flew from its nest.
20.	*seventeen*	"Jacob lived in . . . Egypt *seventeen* years."
21.	*marbles*	Four *marbles* are lost.
22.	*animals*	Some *animals* hibernate all winter.
23.	*all right*	Is it *all right* if he comes?
24.	*greatest*	Obeying God is our *greatest* duty.
25.	*week*	On the first day of the *week*, Jesus arose.

26. *year*   One *year* has twelve months.

27. *cookies*   Are the *cookies* all eaten?

28. *wool*   Clothes made of *wool* are warm.

29. *aren't*   The books *aren't* new any more.

30. *pudding*   We ate chocolate *pudding* for dessert.

31. *different*   Use a *different* color.

32. *holiday*   What was the last *holiday* we had?

33. *remove*   God told Moses to *remove* his shoes.

34. *cents*   Peas cost five *cents* more than beans.

35. *weather*   Warm *weather* helps crops grow.

36. *led*   The shepherd *led* his sheep home.

37. *chase*   I watched the cat *chase* the butterfly.

38. *awhile*   You may rest *awhile;* that will refresh you.

39. *quickly*   Jesus said, "Behold, I come *quickly.*"

40. *presents*   Wise men gave *presents* to Jesus.

41. *cookbook*   Look in the *cookbook* for the recipe.

42. *good-bye*   He waved *good-bye* and rode away.

43. *built*   The wise man *built* his house on a rock.

44. *hungry*   If your enemy is *hungry,* feed him.

45. *chief*   My *chief* desire is to live for God.

For numbers 46–50, write *only* the abbreviations of the words.

46. *Fri.*   *(Friday)*   After Thursday is *Friday*.

For numbers 46–50, write only the abbreviations.

47. *Gen.*   *(Genesis)*   The first book of the Bible is *Genesis*.

48. *mo.*   *(month)*   January is the first *month*.

49. *in.*   *(inch)*   One-twelfth of a foot is an *inch*.

50. *km*   *(kilometer)*   One thousand meters is a *kilometer*.

The Speller Dictionary

Full Pronunciation Key

Abbreviations

adj.	adjective
adv.	adverb
conj.	conjunction
interj.	interjection
n.	noun
prep.	preposition
pron.	pronoun
v.	verb
pl.	plural
sing.	singular

Each entry word in the Speller Dictionary is followed by a phonetic spelling that shows its pronunciation. This pronunciation key lists all the symbols used in the phonetic spellings, and it shows how they should be pronounced.

A heavy accent mark is placed after the syllable that receives the primary accent. A light accent mark follows a syllable with a secondary accent. Observe the primary and secondary accents in the word **pronunciation**: (prə nun′ sē ā′ shən).

Short Vowels
/a/ as in **hat**
/e/ as in **yes**
/i/ as in **sit**
/o/ as in **top**
/u/ as in **bug**

Long Vowels
/ā/ as in **pay**
/ē/ as in **see**
/ī/ as in **by**
/ō/ as in **go**
/yōō/ as in **cube**

Other Vowels and Vowel-*r* Symbols
/ä/ as in **father**
/ô/ as in **saw**
/oi/ as in **boy**
/ŏŏ/ as in **foot**
/ōō/ as in **food**
/ou/ as in **out**
/ə/ the indefinite vowel sound heard in an unaccented syllable, representing any of the five vowels as in **organ, soften, pencil, button, suppose**
/är/ as in **park**
/ûr/ as in **her, fir, bur, earn**, and **worm**
/ər/ as in **hammer**
/âr/ as in **square** or **chair** (allowing /er/ or /ar/)
/îr/ as in **dear** and **deer**
/ôr/ as in **corn**

Consonants
/b/ as in **ball**
/d/ as in **dog**
/f/ as in **fish**
/g/ as in **goat**
/h/ as in **hand**
/j/ as in **jug**
/k/ as in **key**
/l/ as in **leaf**
/m/ as in **mouse**
/n/ as in **nest**
/p/ as in **pie**
/r/ as in **rooster**
/s/ as in **sun**
/t/ as in **turtle**
/v/ as in **vase**
/w/ as in **wagon**
/y/ as in **yarn**
/z/ as in **zebra**
/ch/ as in **chop**
/hw/ as in **wheat**
/ng/ as in **sing**
/sh/ as in **she**
/th/ as in **thin**
/th/ as in **that**
/zh/ as in **measure**

absent   blood

A

ab sent (ab′sənt), *adj.* Away; not present.

act (akt), *v.* 1. To do something. 2. To behave. —*n.* Something done; a deed.

a dore (ə dôr′), *v.,* **a dored, a dor ing.** To love and admire greatly.

a gain (ə gen′), *adv.* Another time; once more.

a gainst (ə genst′), *prep.* In contact with so as to rest or press on.

all right (ôl′rīt′), *adj.* Correct; satisfactory: *That answer is all right. —adv.* In a correct or satisfactory way: *The motor was working all right.*

a mong (ə mung′), *prep.* In with.

an gel (ān′jəl), *n.* A spiritual being that serves as a messenger from God.

an gry (ang′grē), *adj.* Feeling or showing anger; wrathful.

an i mal (an′ə məl), *n.* A living thing that is not a plant or person.

an oth er (ə nuth′ər), *adj.* One more.

an swer (an′sər), *v.* To speak or write in return to a question. —*n.* Words spoken or written in return to a question.

aren't (ärnt). The contraction for **are not.**

a rith me tic (ə rith′mi tik), *n.* A system for working with numbers, which includes addition, subtraction, multiplication, and division.

ar row (ar′ō), *n.* 1. A thin, pointed object that is shot from a bow. 2. A sign (→) used to show direction.

ash (ash), *n.* What remains after something is burned.

Ave. The abbreviation for **Avenue.**

a while (ə hwīl′), *adv.* For a short time.

B

bal loon (bə lōōn′), *n.* A toy made of thin rubber and filled with air or some other gas.

bas ket (bas′kit), *n.* A container made of strips woven together.

beach (bēch), *n.* A flat shore of sand or pebbles along a body of water. —*v.* To pull up on the shore.

bead (bēd), *n.* A small ball or bit of glass, metal, or plastic with a hole through it.

bean (bēn), *n.* 1. A smooth, somewhat flat seed used as a vegetable. 2. A long pod containing such seeds.

beau ti ful (byōō′tə fəl), *adj.* Pleasing to see or hear; delightful.

because (bi kôz′), *conj.* For the reason that; since.

be come (bi kum′), *v.,* **be came, be come, be com ing.** To come to be; to grow to be.

beg (beg), *v.,* **begged, beg ging.** 1. To ask for (food, money, or clothes) as a charity. 2. To ask earnestly for.

be gin ning (bi gin′ing), *v.* Form of **begin.** —*n.* A time when something started; a starting point: *the beginning of the world.*

be lieve (bi lēv′), *v.,* **be lieved, be liev ing.** To accept as being true; to have faith.

bench (bench), *n.* A long, narrow seat.

ber ry (ber′ē), *n., pl.* **ber ries.** Any small, juicy fruit with many seeds.

Beth le hem (beth′li hem′), *n.* A town near Jerusalem where Jesus was born.

Bi ble (bī′bəl), *n.* A book of writings inspired by God; the Holy Scriptures.

bi cy cle (bī′sik′əl), *n.* A two-wheeled vehicle driven by pedaling.

big (big), *adj.,* **big ger, big gest.** Great; large.

birth day (bûrth′dā′), *n.* 1. A day on which a person was born. 2. A yearly returning date of one's birth.

blan ket (blang′kit), *n.* 1. A piece of woven material used as a covering for warmth, usually on a bed. 2. A layer that covers something: *a blanket of snow.*

bless ing (bles′ing), *v.* Form of **bless.** —*n.* 1. The act of one who blesses. 2. A prayer before a meal. 3. Something that brings happiness or prosperity: *count your blessings.*

blew (blōō). Form of **blow.**

blind (blīnd), *adj.* Not able to see. —*n.* Something that blocks light or vision: *a window blind.*

blood (blud), *n.* A red liquid in the veins and arteries.

blow (blō), *v.,* **blew, blown, blow ing.** 1. To move in a stream as the wind does. 2. To move with a stream of air: *The wind blew the leaves.*

bod y (bod′ē), *n., pl.* **bod ies.** 1. The physical structure of a person or an animal. 2. A mass: *a body of water.* 3. The main part of a letter, which gives the message sent.

both er (bo<u>th</u>′ər), *v.* To annoy; distress: *These insects bother me.* —*n.* Something that annoys or distresses: *These insects are a bother.*

bottle (bot′əl), *n.* A container with a narrow neck, used to hold liquids. —*v.,* **bot tled, bot tling.** To put into bottles: *Dairies bottle milk.*

bot tom (bot′əm), *n.* The lowest part.

bought Form of **buy.**

bowl (bōl), *n.* A hollow, rounded dish, usually without handles.

boy (boi), *n.* A male child from birth to about eighteen years.

branch (branch), *n.* A part of a plant growing out from the main stem.

break (brāk), *v.,* **broke, bro ken, break ing.** 1. To cause to go into pieces by using force. 2. To go into pieces; to crack; to burst.

break fast (brek′fəst), *n.* The first meal of the day.

breath (breth), *n.* The air drawn into and forced out of the lungs.

bridge (brij), *n.* Something built to let a road cross a river or similar obstruction.

bright (brīt), *adj.* Giving much light; brilliant.

bring (bring), *v.,* **brought, bring ing.** To take with oneself to a place.

broke (brōk). Form of **break.**

broken (brō′kən). Form of **break.**

brought (brôt). Form of **bring.**

buck le (buk′əl), *n.* A catch or clasp used to hold together the ends of a belt or strap. —*v.,* **buck led, buck ling.** To fasten together with a buckle.

bug gy (bug′ē), *n., pl.* **bug gies.** A light carriage pulled by one horse and having a single seat.

build (bild), *v.,* **built, build ing.** To make by putting materials together; construct.

build ing (bil′ding), *n.* Something that is built, especially a structure such as a house.

built (bilt). Form of **build.**

burn (bûrn), *v.,* **burned** *or* **burnt, burn ing.** Injure or destroy by fire or heat.

bus y (biz′ē), *adj.,* **bus i er, bus i est.** Having plenty to do; working; active.

but ton (but′ən), *n.* A small, flat piece fastened on garments to hold them closed. —*v.* To fasten the buttons of.

buy (bī), *v.,* **bought, buy ing.** To obtain by paying a price; to purchase.

C

calf (kaf), *n., pl.* **calves.** A young cow or bull.

can not (kan′ot *or* ka not′), *v.* Can not; is not able.

care ful (kâr′fəl), *adj.* Watchful of what one does or says.

car ry (kar′ē), *v.,* **car ried, car ry ing.** To take from one place to another.

cash (kash), *n.* Money in the form of coins and bills. —*v.* To exchange for coins and bills: *cash a check.*

catch (kach), *v.,* **caught, catch ing.** To take and hold; to capture.

caught (kôt). Form of **catch.**

cel lar (sel′ər), *n.* An enclosed space underground, often under a building.

cent (sent), *n.* A small copper coin of the United States and Canada; a penny.

cen ti me ter (sen′tə mē′tər), *n.* A unit of length equal to 1/100 of a meter. Also spelled **cen ti me tre.**

chalk board (chôk′bôrd′), *n.* A smooth, hard surface on which to write with chalk.

change (chānj), *v.,* **changed, chang ing.** To make or become different. —*n.* Small coins.

charge (chärj), *v.,* **charged, charg ing.** To ask as a price: *charged 75 cents apiece.*

chase (chās), *v.,* **chased, chas ing.** To go after; to pursue. —*n.* The effort of going after; a pursuit: *gave up after a long chase.*

check (chek), *v.* To find out whether something is true or right; to inspect. —*n.* 1. The act of checking. 2. A paper telling a bank to pay a certain amount of money to a certain person.

cheer (chîr), *n.* Joy; gladness; comfort. —*v.* To make glad; to comfort; to encourage.

cheese (chēz), *n.* A solid food made from milk.

cher ry (cher′ē), *n., pl.* **cher ries.** A small, round, juicy fruit with a stone or pit in it.

chick en (chik′ən), *n.* A hen or rooster.

chief (chēf), *n.* The head of a tribe or group; a leader. —*adj.* Most important; main: *the chief town in the area.*

child (chīld), *n., pl.* **chil dren** (chil′drən). A young boy or girl.

chim ney (chim′nē), *n.* An upright structure that carries away smoke.

choose (chōōz), *v.,* **chose, cho sen, choos ing.** To pick out; to select: *Choose the cake you like best.*

chop (chop), *v.,* **chopped, chop ping.** To cut by striking with something sharp.

Christ mas (kris′məs), *n.* December 25, celebrated as the date of Christ's birth.

church (chûrch), *n.* 1. A building for the worship of God. 2. Public worship of God: *Church started at 7:00.* 3. A group of people with the same religious beliefs: *Our church gave food to poor families.*

cit y (sit′ē), *n., pl.* **cit ies.** A town of considerable size and importance.

class (klas), *n.* 1. A group of persons or things that are alike in some way; a kind; a sort. 2. A group of students who study a subject together.

clay (klā), *n.* A sticky kind of earth that can be easily shaped when wet and hardens when it is dried.

climb (klīm), *v.* To go up, especially by using the hands and feet.

close[1] (klōs), *adj.,* **clos er, clos est.** Near to something; with little space between: *close together.*

close[2] (klōz), *v.,* **closed, clos ing.** To cause to shut: *Close the door.*

cloth (klôth *or* kloth), *n.* Woven or knitted material used to make garments; fabric.

cm The abbreviation for **centimeter.**

coast (kōst), *n.* The land along the sea. —*v.* To move without applying power: *coasted down the hill.*

col or (kul′ər), *n.* A quality such as red, yellow, or blue. —*v.* To give color to, such as by using crayons.

com pa ny (kum′pə nē), *n., pl.* **com pa nies.** 1. A group of people. 2. Visitors; guests: *We had company.* 3. A business; a corporation: *My uncle works for that company.*

cook book (kŏŏk′bŏŏk′), *n.* A book of recipes for preparing various kinds of food.

cook ie *or* **cook y** (kŏŏk′ē), *n., pl.* **cook ies.** A small, flat, sweet cake.

cop y (kop′ē), *n., pl.* **cop ies.** A thing made to be just like another. —*v.,* **cop ied, cop y ing.** To make a copy of.

cost (kôst), *n.* The price required: *The cost of this watch is $10.* —*v.,* **cost, cost ing.** To require as a price: *This watch costs $10.*

cot ton (kot′ən), *n.* 1. Soft, white fibers produced by a certain plant. 2. The plant that produces cotton fibers.

could (kŏŏd), *v.* Was able.

could n't (kŏŏd′ənt). Contraction for **could not.**

count er[1] (koun′tər), *n.* A flat surface where food is served or business transactions are made.

count er[2] (koun′tər), *n.* A person or thing that counts.

count er[3] (koun′tər), *adv.* Contrary; in opposition to: *He acted counter to my suggestion.*

coun try (kun′trē), *n., pl.* **coun tries.** 1. A nation: *the country of France.* 2. The land not in a town: *living in the country.*

cous in (kuz′in), *n.* A son or daughter of one's uncle or aunt.

cov er (kuv′ər), *v.* 1. To put something over: *Cover the child with a blanket.* 2. To hide: *Do not try to cover a mistake.* 3. To go over; to travel: *We covered 400 miles in one day.* —*n.* Something that protects or hides: *a book cover.*

covet   **eighty**

cov et (kuv′it), *v.* To have a wrong desire for (something that belongs to another).

crack (krak), *n.* A split or an opening made by breaking without separating into parts: *a crack in the glass.* —*v.* 1. To break without separating into parts: *cracked the glass.* 3. To make a sudden. sharp noise: *The whip cracked.*

cre ate (krē āt′), *v.,* **cre at ed, cre at ing.** To bring into being (something that did not exist before).

cross (krôs *or* kros), *n.* A form made with two posts or lines that go across each other in the form of the letter *t* or *x.* —*v.* 1. To draw a line across. 2. To move from one side to the other: *crossed the river.*

crowd (kroud), *n.* A large group of people.

curl (kûrl), *v.* To twist into rings or coils. —*n.* A ringlet of hair.

curve (kûrv), *n.* 1. A line with a smooth bend. 2. A bend in a road. —*v.,* **curved, curv ing.** To move in the shape of a curve.

D

Dan. The abbreviation for **Daniel.**

Dan iel (dan′yəl), *n.* One of the books of prophecy in the Old Testament.

death (deth), *n.* The ending of life on earth.

deer (dîr), *n., pl.* **deer.** A swift, graceful animal that has hoofs and chews the cud [from the old English word *dēor,* meaning "wild animal," which later came to mean a certain kind of wild animal].

des ert (dez′ərt), *n.* A region without water and trees.

did n't (did′ənt). The contraction for **did not.**

dif fer ent (dif′ər ənt), *adj.* Not alike; dissimilar.

dirt y (dûr′tē), *adj.,* **dirt i er, dirt i est.** Soiled with dirt; not clean.

dis col ored (dis kul′ərd), *adj.* Having lost its original color.

dis cov er (di skuv′ər), *v.* To learn about for the first time.

dis or der ly (dis ôr′dər lē), *adj.* Not orderly; untidy.

doc tor (dok′tər), *n.* A person trained to treat diseases.

does n't (duz′ənt). The contraction for **does not.**

dol lar (dol′ər), *n.* A unit of money in the United States and various other countries; one hundred cents.

down stairs (doun′stârz′), *adv.* Down the stairs. —*n.* A lower floor of a building.

doz en (duz′ən), *n.* A group of twelve.

Dr. The abbreviation for **Doctor.**

dress (dres), *n.* 1. Clothing, especially outer clothing. 2. An outer garment worn by women and girls. —*v.* To put clothes on.

driv er (drī′vər), *n.* A person who drives.

drop (drop), *n.* A small amount of liquid in a round shape: *a drop of rain.* —*v.,* **dropped, drop ping.** To fall or allow to fall: *The price dropped. Don't drop the eggs.*

drum (drum), *n.* A musical instrument that makes a booming sound when struck. —*v.,* **drummed, drum ming.** To strike or tap again and again: *drummed his fingers on the table.*

dull (dul), *adj.* 1. Not sharp, as a knife. 2. Not bright, as a color. —*v.* To make dull.

dur ing (door′ing *or* dyoor′ing), *prep.* At some time in: *during the night.*

E

ear ly (ûr′lē), *adj., adv.,* **ear li er, ear li est.** Before the usual or proper time: *We had an early dinner. We arrived early.*

earth worm (ûrth′wûrm′), *n.* A reddish brown worm that lives in the soil.

east (ēst), *n.* The direction of the sunrise.

eas y (ē′zē), *adj.* Not hard to do or get.

edge (ej), *n.* 1. A place where something ends; a rim; the brink: *the edge of a cliff.* 2. The cutting side: *the sharp edge of a knife.*

eight een (ā tēn′), *n., adj.* Eight more than ten.

eight y (ā′tē), *n., adj.* Eight times ten.

elephant   fully

el e phant (el′ə fənt), *n.* A large four-footed animal with a trunk [from the Latin word *elephantus*, taken from the Greek word *elephantos*, which originally meant "ivory," the substance composing the tusks of elephants].

en e my (en′ə mē), *n., pl.* **en e mies.** 1. The opposite of a friend; a foe. 2. Something harmful: *Hatred is the enemy of peace.*

enjoy (en joi′), *v.* To have or use with joy; to be happy with.

e nough (i nuf′), *adj.* As many or as much as needed; sufficient: *enough food, enough seats.* —*adv.* Until no more is needed: *has eaten enough.*

Esth. The abbreviation for **Esther.**

Es ther (es′tər), *n.* One of the books of history in the Old Testament.

eve ry where (ev′rē hwâr′), *adv.* At every place.

e vil (ē′vəl), *adj.* Bad; wrong; wicked.

Ex. The abbreviation for **Exodus.**

Ex o dus (ek′sə dəs), *n.* One of the books of the Law in the Old Testament.

Ez ra (ez′rə), *n.* One of the books of history in the Old Testament.

F

fair ly (fâr′lē), *adv.* 1. In a fair manner: *dealt fairly.* 2. Rather; reasonably: *a fairly good crop.*

fam i ly (fam′ə lē), *n., pl.* **fam i lies.** 1. A father, a mother, and their children. 2. A group of similar plants or animals: *Zebras are in the horse family.*

farm er (fär′mər), *n.* A person who raises crops or animals on a farm.

fear ful (fîr′fəl), *adj.* 1. Feeling fear: *a fearful child.* 2. Causing fear: *a fearful storm.*

feath er (feth′ər), *n.* One of the light, thin growths that cover a bird's skin.

fence (fens), *n.* A barrier around something such as a field. —*v.,* **fenced, fenc ing.** To put a fence around.

few (fyōō), *adj.* Not many.

field (fēld), *n.* A piece of land used for crops or pasture.

fifteenth (fif tēnth′), *adj., n.* The next after the fourteenth.

fifth (fifth), *adj., n.* The next after the fourth. 2. One of five equal parts.

fine (fīn), *adj.,* **fin er, fin est.** 1. Very good; excellent. 2. Very small or thin: *a fine wire.*

fin ish (fin′ish), *v.* To bring to an end; to complete.

flash (flash), *n.* A sudden, brief light: *a flash of lightning.* —*v.* To produce a sudden, brief light.

flew (flōō). Form of fly[2].

float (flōt), *v.* To be held up by air, water, or other liquid.

flood (flud), *n.* A great flow of water over what is usually dry land. —*v.* To cover (dry land) with water.

flour (flour), *n.* Fine meal made by grinding and sifting grain.

flow er (flou′ər), *n.* A part of a plant or tree that produces seed; a blossom.

fly[1] (flī), *v.,* **flew, flown, fly ing.** To move through the air by using wings.

fly[2] (flī), *n., pl.* **flies.** Any of a certain group of insects that have two wings.

fol low (fol′ō), *v.* 1. To come after. 2. To heed; to obey: *follow directions.*

foot (fōōt), *n., pl.* **feet.** 1. The end part of a leg. 2. A unit of length equal to 12 inches.

for get (fôr get′), *v.,* **for got, for got ten, for get ting.** To be unable to remember.

for give (fôr giv′), *v.,* **for gave, for giv en, for giv ing.** To give up ill feelings toward (an offender); to pardon.

for ty (fôr′tē), *n., adj.* Four times ten.

Fri. The abbreviation for **Friday.**

Fri day (frī′dā′), *n.* The sixth day of the week.

friend (frend), *n.* A person who knows and likes another.

friend ly (frend′lē), *adj.* Like a friend.

fruit (frōōt), *n.* The product of a tree, bush, or vine, which is usually sweet and good to eat.

ft. The abbreviation for **foot** or **feet.**

ful ly (fōōl′ē), *adv.* Completely; entirely.

G

g The abbreviation for **gram** or **grams.**

gal. The abbreviation for **gallon** or **gallons.**

gal lon (gal′ən), *n.* A unit of liquid measure equal to 4 quarts.

Gen. The abbreviation for **Genesis.**

Genesis (jen′i sis), *n.* The first book of the Law in the Old Testament.

gen tle (jen′təl), *adj.* Mild; not severe, rough, or harsh.

ge og ra phy (jē og′rə fē), *n.* A study of the earth's surface, climates, peoples, and products.

germ (jûrm), *n.* A plant or an animal that can be seen only with a microscope and that may cause disease.

gi ant (jī′ənt), *n.* A person of great size. —*adj.* Having great size: *a giant tree.*

glo ry (glôr′ē), *n., pl.* **glo ries.** 1. Great praise and honor. 2. Heaven.

glove (gluv), *n.* A covering for the hand.

gold en (gōl′dən), *adj.* Made of gold.

good-bye (good bī′), *interj., n.* Farewell.

goose (goos), *n., pl.* **geese.** A bird like a duck, but having a larger size and a longer neck.

grain (grān), *n.* 1. The seed of plants like wheat, oats, and corn. 2. One of the tiny bits of which sand, sugar, or salt are made up. 3. The fine lines that make a pattern in wood.

gram (gram), *n.* A basic unit of weight in the metric system. A nickel weighs about 5 grams.

grand fa ther (grand′fä thər), *n.* The father of one's father or mother.

grand ma (grand′mä′), *n.* A grandmother.

grand pa (grand′pä′), *n.* A grandfather.

grape (grāp), *n.* A small, round fruit that grows in bunches on a vine.

great (grāt), *adj.* Big; large.

great-grand mo ther (grāt′grand′muth′ ər), *n.* The mother of a grandparent.

great-un cle (grāt′ung′kəl), *n.* The brother of a grandparent.

ground (ground), *n.* The surface of the earth; the soil.

grow (grō), *v.,* **grew, grown, grow ing.** 1. To become bigger and more mature: *Plants grow from seeds.* 2. To become: *The weather grew cold.*

guess (ges), *v.* To form an opinion without having full knowledge; to suppose.

H

ham mer (ham′ər), *n.* A tool with a metal head and a handle, used to drive nails.

hand ker chief (hang′kər chif), *n.* A soft square of cloth used for wiping the nose or face.

han dle (han′dəl), *n.* The part of an item made to be held by the hand. —*v.,* **han dled, han dling.** To touch, hold, or use with the hand: *Handle that book carefully.*

hap pen (hap′ən), *v.* To take place; to occur.

have n't (hav′ənt). The contraction for **have not.**

health (helth), *n.* The condition of the body or mind.

health y (hel′thē), *adj.* Having good health.

heap (hēp), *n.* A pile of many things thrown or lying together.

heart (härt), *n.* 1. The body organ that pumps the blood. 2. The center of feelings and desires: *a kind heart.*

hea then (hē′thən), *n.* One who has little or no knowledge of the true God.

heav en (hev′ən), *n.* The place where God and His angels live.

heav y (hev′ē), *adj.* Hard to lift; having much weight.

he'd (hēd). The contraction for **he had** or **he would.**

hel lo (he lō′), *interj.* A call of greeting or surprise.

high way (hī′wā′), *n.* A main public road.

hol i day (hol′i dā′), *n.* A day set aside to celebrate a special event.

hose (hōz), *n.* A flexible tube for carrying liquid or air.

hour (our), *n.* One of the twenty-four equal periods of time in a day; sixty minutes.

hr. The abbreviation for **hour** or **hours.**

huge (hyooj), *adj.* Very large; enormous.

hun dred (hun′drid), *n., adj.* Ten times ten.

hungry   **loaf**

hun gry (hung′grē), *adj.* Feeling a desire or need for food.

hur ry (hûr′ē), *v., **hur ried, hur ry ing.*** To move or act quickly.

I

I'd (īd). The contraction for **I should, I would,** or **I had.**

i dol (īd′əl), *n.* 1. An image that is worshiped as a god. 2. A person or thing that is loved more than God.

I'll (īl). The contraction for **I shall** or **I will.**

in. The abbreviation for **inch** or **inches.**

inch (inch), *n.* A unit of length equal to 1/12 of a foot.

in stead (in sted′), *adv.* In place of (something previously mentioned): *We planned to walk but drove instead.* —**instead of.** Rather than: *drove instead of walking.*

in ter est ing (in′tri sting, *or* in′tə res′ting), *adj.* Holding one's attention; appealing.

in vite (in vīt′), *v., **in vit ed, in vit ing.*** To ask to come.

it's (its). The contraction for **it is** or **it has.**

J

jel ly (jel′ē), *n.* A partly transparent food that is somewhat firm, usually sweet, and commonly spread on bread.

join (join), *v.,* To bring together; to connect.

Josh. The abbreviation for **Joshua.**

Josh u a (josh′o͞o ə), *n.* One of the books of history in the Old Testament.

Judg. The abbreviation for **Judges.**

Judg es (juj′iz), *n.* One of the books of history in the Old Testament.

juice (jo͞os), *n.* The liquid part of fruits, vegetables, and meats.

K

keep (kēp), *v., **kept, keep ing.*** 1. To take care of and protect: *David kept his father's sheep.* 2. To obey; to be faithful to: *keep God's commandments, keep a promise.*

kg The abbreviation for **kilogram.**

kil o gram (kil′ə gram′), *n.* A unit of weight equal to 1,000 grams.

kil o me ter (ki lom′i tər *or* kil′ə mē′tər), *n.* A unit of length equal to 1,000 meters.

kitch en (kich′ən), *n.* A room where food is prepared.

kit ty (kit′ē), *n., pl.* **kit ties.** A pet name for a cat or kitten.

km The abbreviation for **kilometer** or **kilometers.**

L

l The abbreviation for **liter** or **liters.**

lace (lās), *n.* 1. A cord or ribbon used to hold edges together, as of a shoe. 2. A strip with a weblike design used for decoration. —*v.,* **laced, lac ing.** To pull or hold together with a cord or string: *Lace your shoes.*

lad der (lad′ər), *n.* A device having two long sides with rungs in between, used to climb up and down.

lan guage (lang′gwij), *n.* A spoken or written system of communication.

large (lärj), *adj.,* **larg er, larg est.** Big; great.

late (lāt), *adj. or adv.,* **lat er, lat est.** After the usual or proper time: *We had a late dinner. We arrived late.*

laugh (laf), *v.* To make the sounds and movements of one who is happy or amused.

lawn (lôn), *n.* A piece of grassy land, usually mowed and often lying around a house; a yard.

lb. The abbreviation for **pound** or **pounds.**

lead (lēd), *v., **led, lead ing.*** 1. To show the way by going ahead of. 2. To provide a way to: *Hard work leads to success.*

les son (les′ən), *n.* Something to be learned.

let ter (let′ər), *n.* 1. One of the alphabetic symbols used to write words. 2. A written or printed message.

li ter (lē′tər), *n.* A basic unit of volume in the metric system. A liter is slightly more than a quart. Also spelled **litre.**

load (lōd), *n.* Something that is carried; a burden.

loaf (lōf), *n., pl.* **loaves.** A mass of bread baked as one piece.

lock (lok), *n.* A device for fastening, usually needing a key to open it. —*v.* To fasten with a lock.

low (lō), *adj.* 1. Not high or tall: *a low hill.* 2. Near the ground: *a low opening.* —*adv.* At or to a low position: *stooped low, flew low.*

M

m The abbreviation for **meter** or **meters.**

mar ble (mär′bəl), *n.* A small ball of clay, glass, or marble, used in games.

mar ket (mär′kit), *n.* A public place where goods are sold.

match[1] (mach), *n.* Something that is very much like another: *These colors are a good match.* —*v.* To be alike; to go together: *These shoes do not match.*

match[2] (mach), *n.* A short, slender piece of wood or cardboard tipped with a mixture that makes fire when rubbed on a rough surface.

melt (melt), *v.* To turn into a liquid by applying heat.

Men non ite (men′ə nīt′), *n.* Member of a religious group that started from the Anabaptist movement in the 1500s.

mer cy (mûr′sē), *n., pl.* **mer cies.** More kindness than one deserves; kindness beyond what can be claimed or expected.

me ter (mē′tər), *n.* A basic unit of length in the metric system. A meter equals about 39 1/3 inches. Also spelled **metre.**

mi. The abbreviation for **mile** or **miles.**

mid dle (mid′əl), *n.* A place that is the same distance from each end or side; the center.

might[1] (mīt), *n.* Power; strength: *Try with all your might.*

might[2] (mīt), *helping v.* Used to express possibility: *It might rain today.*

mile (mīl), *n.* A unit of length equal to 5,280 feet.

min is ter (min′i stər), *n.* A church leader; a pastor.

min ute (min′it), *n.* One of the sixty equal parts of an hour; 60 seconds.

Miss (mis), *n.* A title for a woman or girl who is not married.

mix (miks), *v.* To put together to form one mass; to combine.

mo. The abbreviation for **month** or **months.**

Mon. The abbreviation for **Monday.**

Mon day (mun′dā′), *n.* The second day of the week.

month (munth), *n.* One of the twelve parts into which a year is divided.

moon light (mōōn′līt′), *n.* The light from the moon.

moun tain (moun′tən), *n.* A very high hill.

mouse (mous), *n., pl.* **mice.** A small gnawing animal.

mouth (mouth), *n.* 1. The opening through which a person or animal takes in food. 2. An opening that suggests a mouth: *the mouth of a cave.*

Mr. The abbreviation for **Mister,** a title used before a man's name.

Mrs. The abbreviation for **Mistress,** a title used before a married woman's name.

mud dy (mud′ē), *adj.* Having much mud; covered with mud.

mule (myōōl), *n.* An animal that is half horse and half donkey.

mu sic (myōō′zik), *n.* A pleasing arrangement of sounds, which usually includes melody and rhythm.

my self (mī self′), *pron., pl.* **our selves.** 1. Used with **I** or **me** to make a statement stronger: *I myself wrote that letter.* 2. Used instead of **I** or **me** to show that the doer of an action is also the receiver: *I saw myself in the mirror.*

N

naugh ty (nô′tē), *adj.* Not behaving well; not obedient.

near ly (nîr′lē), *adv.* Almost.

nee dle (nēd′əl), *n.* A slender tool with a sharp point and a hole to pass thread through, used in sewing.

news pa per (nōōz′pā′pər *or* nyōōz′pā′pər), *n.* Sheets of paper printed every day or week, telling the news and carrying advertisements.

nine teen (nīn tēn′), *n., adj.* Nine more than ten.

nine ty (nīn′tē), *n., adj.* Nine times ten.

noise   **pocketbook**

noise (noiz), *n.* A sound, usually unpleasant or undesirable.

north (nôrth), *n.* The direction toward the North Pole.

Num. The abbreviation for **Numbers.**

Num bers (num′bərz), *n.* One of the books of the Law in the Old Testament.

nurse (nûrs), *n.* A person who takes care of the sick, the old, or the very young. —*v.,* **nursed, nurs ing.** To take care of (a sick, old, or very young person): *nursed him back to health.*

O

oat meal (ōt′mēl′), *n.* Oats made into meal.

o cean (ō′shən), *n.* A great body of salt water.

o'clock (ə klok′). The contraction for **of the clock,** used in telling time: *six o'clock.*

of ten (ô′fən *or* ôf′tən), *adv.* Many times; frequently.

old (ōld), *adj.* Not young; having been for some time.

o pen (ō′pən), *adj.* Not shut. —*v.* To make or became open: *We opened a path through the snow.*

or ange (ôr′inj), *n.* 1. A round, juicy fruit that grows in warm regions. 2. The color of the orange, made by mixing red and yellow.

or der (ôr′dər), *v.* To tell what to do; to give a command. —*n.* 1. A direction; a command: *received an order.* 2. An organized arrangement: *put things in order.*

oth er (uth′ər), *adj.* Not the same; different: *other friends.* —*pron.* Not the same one; a different person or thing: *one hand or the other.*

ounce (ouns), *n.* A unit of weight equal to 1/16 of a pound.

own er (ō′nər), *n.* One who owns.

oz. The abbreviation for **ounce** or **ounces.**

P

pack (pak), *n.* A bundle of things wrapped together. —*v.* To put together as a bundle or in a container: *pack a suitcase.*

pack age (pak′ij), *n.* A bundle of things packed together.

page (pāj), *n.* One side of a sheet of paper.

paint ing (pānt′ing), *v.* Form of **paint.** —*n.* A picture made with paint.

pair (pâr), *n.* A set of two: *a pair of shoes.*

pa per (pā′pər), *n.* A sheet of material used for writing and drawing.

par ent (pâr′ənt), *n.* A father or mother.

patch (pach), *n.* A small piece of material used to mend a hole. —*v.* To put a patch on; to mend.

pea (pē), *n.* 1. A round seed that grows in a pod, used as a vegetable. 2. A plant that produces such seeds.

peace (pēs), *n.* Freedom from strife; harmony.

peach (pēch), *n.* A round, juicy fruit with a hard stone inside.

pen cil (pen′səl), *n.* A long, thin, usually rounded writing or drawing tool containing graphite or crayon. —*v.* To mark or write with a pencil.

pen ny (pen′ē), *n., pl.* **pen nies.** A copper coin worth one cent, used in the United States and Canada.

per son (pûr′sən), *n.* A man, woman, or child.

pic nic (pik′nik), *n.* A meal eaten outdoors.

pic ture (pik′chər), *n.* A drawing, painting, or photograph.

piece (pēs), *n.* One of the parts into which something is divided.

pil low (pil′ō), *n.* A bag filled with soft material to support the head when resting.

pint (pīnt), *n.* A unit of liquid or dry measure equal to half a quart.

pitch[1] (pich), *n.* A black, sticky material made from tar.

pitch[2] (pich), *v.* To throw; to toss.

plan (plan), *n.* A way of making or doing something that is worked out beforehand. —*v.,* **planned, plan ning.** To think out a plan.

plant (plant), *n.* A living thing that is not a person or an animal. —*v.* To put in the ground to grow: *Farmers plant seeds.*

plow (plou), *n.* A device for turning soil over. —*v.* To turn over (soil) with a plow.

pock et book (pok′it bo͝ok′), *n.* 1. A woman's purse. 2. A case for carrying money or papers in a pocket.

po em (pō′əm), *n.* An appealing arrangement of words in orderly lines. often with rhythm and rhyme.

point (point), *n.* 1. A sharp end: *the point of a needle.* 2. A specific place: *The lines cross at this point.* —*v.* To turn straight toward; to aim: *The fireman pointed his hose at the flames.*

pool (pōol), *n.* A small pond.

porch (pôrch), *n.* A roofed platform at the entrance of a building.

pound (pound), *n.* A unit of weight equal to 16 ounces.

praise (prāz), *v., praised, prais ing.* To worship in words or song; to express adoration.

prayer (prâr), *n.* 1. The act of speaking to God. 2. A form of words used in praying: *the Lord's Prayer.*

preach (prēch), *v.* To deliver a sermon on; to proclaim: *preach the Gospel.*

preach er (prē′chər), *n.* A person who preaches; a pastor; a minister.

pres ent[1] (prez′ənt), *adj.* 1. At this time; now: *the present moment.* 2. Being at a certain place: *every pupil was present.* —*n.* 1. The time now here; this time: *not working at the present.* 2. A gift: *a birthday present.*

pre sent[2] (pri zent′), *v.* To come or give formally: *The Israelites presented themselves before God. They presented their offerings.*

print (print), *v.* To use type to stamp words on: *print a book.* —*n.* Printed letters or other symbols: *words in large print.*

Prov. The abbreviation for **Proverbs.**

Prov erbs (prov′ərbz′), *n.* One of the books of poetry in the Old Testament.

pt. The abbreviation for **pint** or **pints.**

pud ding (pŏod′ing), *n.* A soft, cooked food, usually sweet, served as a dessert.

puff (puf), *v.* To blow with short, quick blasts. —*n.* Something puffed out: *a puff of smoke.*

pull (pŏol), *v.* To move (something) toward oneself, usually with force or effort. —*n.* The action of pulling: *gave a hard pull.*

pump (pump), *n.* A device for forcing liquid, air, or gas to move from one place to another: *a water pump.* —*v.* To move (liquid, air, or gas) by using a pump.

pun ish (pun′ish), *v.* To cause pain or loss because of wrongdoing.

pup py (pup′ē), *n., pl.* **pup pies.** A young dog.

Q

qt. The abbreviation for **quart** or **quarts.**

quart (kwôrt), *n.* A unit of liquid or dry measure equal to 1/4 gallon.

ques tion (kwes′chən), *n.* An expression of asking in order to find out. —*v.* To ask a question.

quick ly (kwik′lē), *adv.* In a fast manner; swiftly.

R

rab bit (rab′it), *n.* An animal with soft fur and long ears.

rain y (rā′nē), *adj.* Having much rain: *April is a rainy month.*

raise (rāz), *v., raised, rais ing.* To lift up; to cause to go up: *Raise your hand.*

rath er (ra*th*′ər), *adv.* More willingly: *I would rather go today than tomorrow.*

Rd. The abbreviation for **Road.**

reach (rēch), *v.* To try to touch or grasp. —*n.* An area within which one is able to get something: *out of my reach.*

read y (red′ē), *adj.* Prepared for immediate action or use: *Lunch is ready.*

rea son (rē′zən) *n.* 1. A cause; an explanation: *the reason for her absence.* 2. Soundness of mind: *Nebuchadnezzar lost his reason for a time.* —*v.* To decide by using the mind: *reasoned that the statement must be true.*

re ceive (ri sēv′), *v., re ceived, re ceiv ing.* To be given; to get; to obtain.

re cess (rē′ses′), *n.* A temporary stopping of an activity.

re mem ber (ri mem′bər), *v.* To call to mind: *I cannot remember the man's name.*

re move (ri mŏov′), *v., re moved, re mov ing.* To move (something) from a place: *Remove your hat.*

ribbon   **size**

rib bon (rib′ən), *n.* A strip or band, usually of a fine material such as silk or satin.

ring[1] (ring), *n.* A circle: *The children stood in a ring.*

ring[2] (ring), *v.,* **rang, rung, ring ing.** To give forth a clear sound like that of a bell: *I heard the telephone ring.*

rob in (rob′in), *n.* An American bird with a dark back and a reddish breast.

rod (rod), *n.* A thin, straight bar of metal or wood.

root[1] (rōōt *or* rŏŏt), *n.* The part of a plant that grows down into the soil.

root[2] (rōōt *or* rŏŏt), *v.* To dig with the snout: *The pigs were rooting the garden.*

rub (rub), *v.,* **rubbed, rub bing.** To move one thing back and forth against another.

rush (rush), *v.* To move with speed and force.

S

sack (sak), *n.* A large bag made of coarse cloth.

sad (sad), *adj.,* **sad der, sad dest.** Not happy; sorrowful.

sal va tion (sal vā′shən), *n.* The saving of the soul; the deliverance from sin and the punishment for sin.

2 Sam. The abbreviation for **2 Samuel.**

2 Sam u el (sek′ənd sam′yōō əl), *n.* One of the books of history in the Old Testament.

Sat. The abbreviation for **Saturday.**

Sat ur day (sat′ər dā′), *n.* The seventh day of the week.

say (sā), *v.,* **said, say ing, says** (sez). To express with words; to declare.

scare (skâr), *v.,* **scared, scar ing.** To frighten.

school house (skōōl′hous′), *n.* A building where school is held.

seal[1] (sēl), *n.* An official design stamped on something to show ownership or authority. —*v.* 1. To mark with a seal. 2. To enclose tightly: *seal food in jars.*

seal[2] (sēl), *n.* A sea animal with large flippers.

see saw (sē′sô′), *n.* An outdoor toy made of a plank resting on a raised center support so that the ends can move up and down.

sev en (sev′ən), *n., adj.* One more than six.

sev en teen (sev′ən tēn′), *n., adj.* Seven more than ten.

sew (sō), *v.,* **sewed, sewed** *or* **sewn, sew ing.** To fasten with stitches.

shake (shāk), *v.,* **shook, shak en, shak ing.** To move quickly back and forth.

shape (shāp), *n.* A form; an appearance. —*v.,* **shaped, shap ing.** To give a certain form to.

share (shâr), *n.* The part belonging to one person: *Do your share of the work.* —*v.,* **shared, shar ing.** 1. To take part: *Everyone shared in cleaning the yard.* 2. To give (part of something) to someone as an act of kindness: *John shared his lunch with his friend.*

sharp (shärp), *adj.* 1. Having a thin cutting edge; not dull: *a sharp knife.* 2. With a sudden change of direction: *a sharp turn.* 3. Detecting things quickly: *sharp ears.*

shell (shel), *n.* The hard outer covering of eggs, nuts, and certain animals.

shine (shīn), *v.,* **shone** *or* **shined, shin ing.** To send out light.

ship (ship), *n.* A large vessel for travel on water. —*v.,* **shipped, ship ping.** To send from one place to another by ship or some other means of transportation.

shop (shop), *n.* A place where things are made, repaired, or sold. —*v.,* **shopped, shop ping.** To visit stores to look at or to buy things.

shore (shôr), *n.* The land at the edge of a sea, lake, or large river.

should (shŏŏd), *helping v.* Used to express duty, uncertainty, and other things: *You should do your best. I took an umbrella in case it should rain.*

silver (sil′vər), *n.* A shiny, white, precious metal.

since (sins), *prep.* From a past time until now: *We have not met since then.* —*conj.* Because: *Since you feel tired, you should rest.*

sir (sûr), *n.* A title of respect or honor used for a man.

six teen (sik stēn′), *n., adj.* Six more than ten.

six ty (siks′tē), *adj., n.* Six times ten.

size (sīz), *n.* The amount of space a thing takes up: *The two boys are of the same size.*

skate

skate (skāt), *n.* A shoe with a blade or rollers attached so that a person can glide over ice or a smooth surface. —*v.,* **skat ed, skat ing.** To move along on skates.

skin (skin), *n.* The layer that covers the body. —*v.,* **skinned, skin ning.** To take the skin off.

sleep (slēp), *n.* A rest taken in an unconscious or a partly conscious state. —*v.,* **slept, sleep ing.** To rest the body and mind through sleep.

sleep y (slē′pē), *adj.* Ready to sleep; drowsy.

slip (slip), *v.,* **slipped, slip ping.** 1. To move smoothly and quietly: *We slipped out of the room.* 2. To slide suddenly out of place: *The knife slipped and cut my finger.* —*n.* A small piece: *a slip of paper.*

slow ly (slō′lē), *adv.* In a slow manner.

small (smôl), *adj.* Not large; little.

smell (smel), *v.* To detect an odor by using the nose: *Can you smell the smoke?* —*n.* 1. The sense of smelling: *Smell is keener in dogs than in men.* 2. An odor: *A rose has a sweet smell.*

smooth (smōoth), *adj.* 1. Having an even surface like glass; flat; level. 2. Having an even quality; not rough: *a smooth ride.*

so fa (sō′fə), *n.* A long, upholstered seat or couch having a back and arms.

some where (sum′hwâr′), *adv.* At or to some place.

soon (sōon), *adv.* Before long; shortly.

soup (sōop), *n.* A food made by boiling vegetables, meat, or fish in water or other liquid.

south (south), *n.* The direction toward the South Pole.

space (spās), *n.* A place or room: *Is there enough space in the car?* —*v.,* **spaced, spac ing.** To separate with spaces: *Space your words evenly when you write.*

spoil (spoil), *v.* To damage beyond recovery; ruin.

square (skwâr), *n.* A figure with four equal sides and four right angles. —*adj.* Having the shape of a square: *a square box.*

squir rel (skwûr′əl), *n.* A small, bushy-tailed animal.

St. The abbreviation for **Street** or **Saint**: *Main St., St. Louis.*

staff (staf), *n.* 1. A stick; a pole; a rod. 2. Five lines and four spaces on which music is written.

stage (stāj), *n.* 1. A raised platform for speaking or performing. 2. A step in the development of something: *a butterfly in the pupa stage.*

stand (stand), *v.,* **stood, stand ing.** To be upright on one's feet.

sta tion (stā′shən), *n.* 1. An appointed place: *The guard took his station at the door.* 2. A regular stopping place: *the bus station.*

steal (stēl), *v.,* **stole, sto len, steal ing.** To take wrongly what belongs to someone else.

steam (stēm), *n.* The water that has been heated to form a vapor. —*v.* To give off steam: *The cup of coffee was steaming.*

steel (stēl), *n.* Iron mixed with carbon to make it very hard, strong, and tough.

stir (stûr), *v.,* **stirred, stir ring.** 1. To move: *The wind stirs the leaves.* 2. To mix by moving around with a spoon or some other device: *stir the cake batter.*

stock ing (stok′ing), *n.* A close-fitting, knitted covering for the foot and leg.

sto ry[1] (stôr′ē), *n., pl.* **sto ries.** An account of some happening: *read the story of Jonah.*

sto ry[2] (stôr′ē), *n., pl.* **sto ries.** A set of rooms on the same floor of a building: *That house has two stories.*

strange (strānj), *adj.* 1. Not known or seen before; unfamiliar: *a strange sound.* 2. Out of place; not at home: *The poor child felt strange in the palace.*

straw (strô), *n.* Dry stems of grain left after threshing.

stream (strēm), *n.* A flow of liquid or gas. —*v.* To move in a flow.

strike (strīk), *v.,* **struck, struck** *or* **strick en, strik ing.** To hit sharply.

study (stud′ē), *v.,* **stud ied, stud y ing.** To try to learn: *We studied our lesson.* —*n., pl.* **stud ies.** A room for studying, reading, or writing: *The minister was reading in his study.*

sud den ly (sud′ən lē), *adv.* In a sudden manner; unexpectedly.

suf fer (suf′ər), *v.* 1. To have pain or grief. 2. To allow; to permit.

sug ar (shŏŏg′ər), *n.* A sweet substance usually made from sugar cane or sugar beets.

suit (sōōt), *n.* A set of clothes to be worn together. —*v.* To be satisfactory; to be workable: *It did not suit for us to go.*

Sun. The abbreviation for **Sunday.**

Sun day (sun′dā′), *n.* The first day of the week, which Christians observe as the day of rest and worship.

sup ply (sə plī′), *v.,* **sup plied, sup ply ing.** To furnish; to provide: *The school supplies books for the children.* —*n., pl.* **sup plies.** An amount ready for use; a stock: *a supply of food.*

sur prise (sər prīz′), *n.* Something unexpected. —*v.,* **sur prised, sur pris ing.** To catch unprepared; to come upon suddenly.

T

teach (tēch), *v.,* **taught, teach ing.** To give knowledge; to help to learn.

teach er (tē′chər), *n.* A person who teaches.

team (tēm), *n.* Two or more people or animals doing something together.

tear[1] (târ), *v.,* **tore, torn, tear ing.** To pull apart by force: *Don't tear the page.*

tear[2] (tîr), *n.* A drop of salty water coming from the eye.

tem ple (tem′pəl), *n.* A special building used for the worship ceremonies.

term (tûrm), *n.* 1. The length of time appointed for something: *a school term.* 2. A word or phrase with a specific meaning: *a term used in science.*

ter ri ble (ter′ə bəl), *adj.* Causing great fear; dreadful: *a terrible storm.*

thank ful (thangk′fəl), *adj.* Feeling thanks; grateful.

Thanks giv ing (thangks giv′ing), *n.* A holiday on which to give special thanks for God's kindness through the year.

that's (thats). The contraction for **that is** or **that has.**

their (thâr), *adj.* Of them; belonging to them.

thick (thik), *adj.* 1. With much space between opposite sides: *a thick book.* 2. Having a quality that makes stirring difficult: *thick glue.*

thin (thin), *adj.,* **thin ner, thin nest.** 1. With little space between opposite sides: *a thin layer.* 2. Having a quality that makes stirring easy; runny: *thin syrup.*

thine (thīn), *pron.* Belonging to thee: *Thine is the kingdom.*

think (thingk), *v.,* **thought, think ing.** 1. To use the mind: *Think carefully before answering.* 2. To have an opinion; to suppose: *Do you think it will rain?*

thir teen (thûr tēn′), *n., adj.* Three more than ten.

thir ty (thûr′tē), *n., adj.* Three times ten.

thou sand (thou′zənd), *n., adj.* Ten hundred.

through (thrōō), *prep.* From end to end of; from side to side of; between the parts of: *The carpenter drove a nail through the board.*

throw (thrō), *v.,* **threw, thrown, throw ing.** To cast; to toss; to hurl: *throw a ball.*

Thur. The abbreviation for **Thursday.**

Thurs day (thûrz′dā′), *n.* The fifth day of the week.

ti ger (tī′gər), *n.* A large, fierce animal of Asia that has dull-yellow fur striped with black.

1 Tim. The abbreviation for **1 Timothy.**

1 Tim o thy (fûrst′ tim′ə thē), *n.* One of the Epistles in the New Testament.

to geth er (tə geth′ər), *adv.* With each other; in company: *The girls were walking together.*

tomb (tōōm), *n.* A grave or burial vault for a dead body, often above the ground.

to mor row (tə môr′ō *or* tə mor′ō), *n.* The day after today. —*adv.* On the day after today: *finish tomorrow.*

tooth (tōōth), *n., pl.* **teeth.** Hard, bonelike part in the mouth, used for chewing.

touch (tuch), *v.* To put part of the body against and feel.

track   whenever

track (trak), *n.* 1. A rail or pair of rails for trains to run on. 2. A footprint: *bear tracks.* —*v.* To make footprints on.

trav el (trav′əl), *v.* To go from one place to another. —*n.* The act or method of going from one place to another.

Trin i ty (trin′i tē), *n.* The union of the Father, Son, and Holy Ghost as one God.

trou ble (trub′əl), *n.* 1. Distress; difficulty; hardship. 2. An extra effort: *Take the trouble to do neat work.* —*v.,* **troubled, trou bling.** To cause distress or difficulty for; to bother: *She is troubled by headaches.*

tru ly (trōo′lē), *adv.* In a true manner; rightly; faithfully.

trunk (trungk), *n.* 1. The main stem of a tree. 2. An elephant's snout. 3. A storage chest. 4. The compartment at the back of a car for carrying things.

truth (trōoth), *n.* That which is true: *Tell the truth.*

try (trī), *v.,* **tried, try ing.** To attempt; to endeavor.

Tues. The abbreviation for **Tuesday.**

Tues day (tōoz′dā′ *or* tyōoz′dā′), *n.* The third day of the week.

tu lip (tōo′lip *or* tyōo′lip), *n.* A spring flower with a cup-shaped bloom.

tune (tōon *or* tyōon), *n.* The music for a song; a melody.

tur key (tûr′kē), *n.* A large, North American bird used for food.

tur tle (tûr′təl), *n.* An animal having a soft body enclosed in a hard shell into which many kinds can draw their head and legs.

twelve (twelv), *n., adj.* One more than eleven.

twice (twīs), *adv.* Two times; doubly: *twice as much.*

twin kle (twing′kəl), *v.,* **twin kled, twin kling.** To shine with quick little gleams; to glimmer.

U

un less (un les′), *conj.* If not: *We shall go unless it rains.*

un like (un līk′), *adj.* Not like; different: *two unlike problems.*

un paint ed (un pān′tid), *adj.* Not painted.

until (un til′), *conj.* Up to the time when: *He waited until the sun had set.*

V

va ca tion (vā kā′shən), *n.* Freedom from school, work, or other duties.

veg e ta ble (vej′tə bəl *or* vej′i tə bəl), *n.* 1. A plant raised for seeds, leaves, roots, or other parts that can be used as food. 2. A part of such a plant that is eaten.

vi o let (vī′ə lit), *n.* 1. A small spring flower with a purple, blue, yellow, or white bloom. 2. A bluish purple color.

vis it (viz′ət), *v.* To come or go to see: *I shall visit my aunt next week.*

W

wa fer (wā′fər), *n.* A thin cake or biscuit.

want (wont), *v.* To wish for; to desire.

was n't (wuz′ənt), Contraction for **was not.**

watch (woch), *v.* To look at steadily or carefully: *We watched the kittens playing.* —*n.* A small device for telling time.

wax (waks), *n.* An oily or greasy substance such as that used by bees to make honeycombs. —*v.* To apply wax to: *waxed the floor.*

wear (wâr), *v.,* **wore, worn, wear ing.** 1. To have on for clothing. 2. To damage by friction: *worn tires.*

weather (weth′ər), *n.* The condition of the outside air at a certain time and place: *warm weather.*

Wed. The abbreviation for **Wednesday.**

Wednes day (wenz′dā′), *n.* The fourth day of the week.

weed (wēd), *n.* A useless or troublesome plant.

week (wēk), *n.* Seven days one after another.

we're (wîr). The contraction for **we are.**

west (west), *n.* The direction of the sunset.

when ev er (hwen ev′ər), *conj.* At any time that: *Please come whenever you can.*

which

zone

which (hwich), *adj.* Used in asking questions: *Which books are yours?* —*pron.* Used in asking questions, in telling *what one*, and in connecting word groups in sentences: *Which is your book? Choose which you like best. This is Mother's book, which I brought.*

whis tle (hwis′əl), *v.,* **whis tled, whis tling.** To make a clear, shrill sound: *The boy whistled for his dog.* —*n.* A device for whistling.

whole (hōl), *adj.* Having all its parts; complete; entire: *a whole set of dishes.*

whose (hōōz), *pron.* Of or belonging to whom or which: *Whose coat is this?*

win dow (win′dō), *n.* An opening to let light or air into a building.

wis dom (wiz′dəm), *n.* The quality of being wise; knowledge and good judgment based on experience.

wk. The abbreviation for **week** or **weeks.**

wolf (wŏŏlf), *n., pl.* **wolves.** A wild animal somewhat like a dog.

wo man (wŏŏm′ən), *n., pl.* **wo men** (wim′in). A female adult person.

won der (wun′dər), *v.* To be curious about; to wish to know: *I wonder what time it is.* —*n.* Something that causes surprise or admiration: *We saw many wonders on our trip.*

won't (wōnt). The contraction for **will not.**

wood en (wŏŏd′ən), *adj.* Made of wood.

wool (wŏŏl), *n.* 1. The soft, curly hair or fur that grows on sheep and some other animals. 2. The yarn, cloth, or garments made of wool: *wearing wool in cold weather.*

world (wûrld), *n.* 1. The earth: *Ships can sail around the world.* 2. Things of this life and people devoted to them: *Christians live differently from the world.*

would n't (wŏŏd′ənt). The contraction for **would not.**

Y

yard[1] (yärd), *n.* A unit of length equal to 36 inches or 3 feet.

yard[2] (yärd), *n.* A piece of land near or around buildings, often covered with grass.

yd. The abbreviation for **yard** or **yards.**

year (yîr), *n.* A unit of time equal to twelve months.

yoke (yōk), *n.* 1. A wooden frame for fastening two work animals together. 2. A pair of animals fastened together with a yoke: *watched a yoke of oxen.*

young (yung), *adj.* In the early part of life; not old.

your (yŏŏr *or* yôr), *adj.* Belonging to you: *Wash your hands.*

you're (yŏŏr). The contraction for **you are.**

your self (yŏŏr self′ *or* yôr self′), *pron., pl.* **your selves.** 1. Used instead of **you** to make a statement stronger: *Do the work yourself.* 2. Used instead of **you** to show that the doer of an action is also the receiver: *Did you hurt yourself?*

yr. The abbreviation for **year** or **years.**

Z

zone (zōn), *n.* An area or district, especially in a city or town.